# SAVAGE SETS!

# SAVAGE SETS!

## The Ultimate Pre-exhaust Pump Out

*Robert Kennedy*

**Sterling Publishing Co., Inc.   New York**
Cassell PLC   London, England

**Library of Congress Cataloging-in-Publication Data**

Kennedy, Robert, 1938-
    Savage sets! : the ultimate pre-exhaust pump out / Robert Kennedy.
        p.      cm.
    ISBN 0-8069-6895-8
    1. Bodybuilding.      I. Title.
    GV546.5.K4628   1989                                    89-38783
    646.7'5—dc20                                            CIP

**Drawings by Candace Olsen**

**Edited by Carol Palmer and Robert Hernandez**

**Designed by Jim Anderson**

Copyright © 1989 by Robert Kennedy
Published by Sterling Publishing Co., Inc.
387 Park Avenue South, New York, N.Y. 10016
Distributed in Canada by Sterling Publishing
% Canadian Manda Group, P.O. Box 920, Station U
Toronto, Ontario, Canada M8Z 5P9
Distributed in Great Britain and Europe by Cassell PLC
Artillery House, Artillery Row, London SW1P 1RT, England
Distributed in Australia by Capricorn Ltd.
P.O. Box 665, Lane Cove, NSW 2066
*Manufactured in the United States of America*
*All rights reserved*
Sterling ISBN 0-8069-6895-8 Paper

# CONTENTS

Bodybuilding's massive Phil Hill

# INTRODUCTION

If you ask the average person how to build a superior body, chances are he'll tell you to work out with weights. That much is known and understood well enough. Yet, modern bodybuilding has progressed far beyond working out casually with barbells and dumbbells to produce results. Today it's a science, and with all the training and nutritional information available, the sport is fast becoming an *exact* science.

Bodybuilding is full of principles and techniques. Some trainers can legitimately claim to have invented certain bodybuilding methods. Frequently, individuals didn't actually invent the methods, but only applied names to existing techniques and publicized them. No one could possibly claim to have invented the cheating principle, strict or rest-pause training, peak contraction, half, pyramid, slow-motion, or negative reps, continuous tension, straight or compound sets, or even supersets. All these methods were practiced over 100 years ago. I have the reference manuals, books, and old issues of physical-culture magazines to prove it.

John Terilli

That's not to say there's nothing new in the world of bodybuilding. Almost every month a new, sophisticated progressive-resistance machine comes on the market. Even the computer age is upon us. Sensitive, electronic sensors and programs, which are attached to specialized apparatus, are dictating the resistance to use and the ideal number of reps for muscle growth. Much of this modern technology is in its infancy and hasn't yet proved how effective it actually is, but the writing's on the wall.

Many bodybuilders are aware that I invented the pre-exhaust technique back in 1960. I worked out the theory in my head long before putting it into practice. Necessity is the mother of invention; and at the age of twenty-one, after six years of hard training, I still couldn't add any real muscle mass to my shoulders. The usual way of building your shoulders during those days was to perform the military barbell press followed by an isolation movement such as the dumbbell lateral raise. This worked for most people, and indeed, it worked for me to a degree. However hard I tried, I couldn't build the kind of deltoid mass that I considered impressive. Big, rotund, melon-sized delts are, let's admit it, rare. But for those lucky few who possess them, they are appealing beyond words.

Being an art student, specializing in oil painting and sculpture, I had easy access to a pair of calipers. Periodically, I would measure my shoulder width, which never changed: a mediocre twenty-one inches. I read in magazines that the shoulders of Mr. America Steve Reeves measured a full twenty-four inches across, while Mr. America Mickey Hargitay could boast an honest measurement of twenty-six inches. This all seemed very impressive to me.

I was spurred on to lifting heavier weights and tried just about every deltoid exercise in the book. I did very strict upright rows and presses behind my neck with 160 pounds, both for eight reps. I performed lateral raises with fifty-pound dumbbells. My best achievement was the single-arm press, which I did with a 155-pound barbell simply because I didn't have dumbbells that were over 100 pounds. I did this lift managing five to six reps every set, but not a strict movement. As I pressed the bar upward, I would bend in the opposite direction to "cheat" the weight skyward. What was the result of all this iron tossing? Zero growth!

Paul Jean Guillaume has super shoulders.

Vince Comerford shows off his biceps.

What upset me most was the fact that I just could not get my shoulders to pump, ache, burn, or even to be sore the next day. Sure enough, I kept the muscle growth I had already built, but I couldn't make additional gains in actual size. After more experimentation, I did find a new method that gave me an increase, but it was still neither dramatic nor satisfying. I would perform six sets of six to eight reps of presses behind my neck. Then I followed this quickly with ten sets of twenty reps of cable lateral raises, using two rubber cables with one handle placed under each foot. After the heavy presses, which stressed the muscle cells, the high-rep rubber-cable laterals really worked my delts. Even so, after the first few workouts, the pump became less and less, and my delts still weren't sore the morning after.

I clearly remember placing two folded hand-kerchiefs under my T-shirt on my deltoids, which added about a half inch to the width of each one. When I looked in the mirror, it made me look like Hercules unchained! I concluded that even the smallest of gains on my deltoids would improve my appearance 100 percent. I clearly defined the problem as needing to work my deltoids more vigorously than ever before. How could I get to the deepest fibers? How could I pulverize them so that they had absolutely no alternative but to grow?

The answer came to me one night. I would work the deltoid caps first by tiring them with an isolation movement such as the lateral raise, and then go to the limit with a combination exercise such as the press behind neck. I figured that the already fatigued deltoids would work hard to keep up with the demand placed on them during the combination movement. In order to keep pace with the triceps muscles, the pre-exhausted deltoids would have to really dig down deep to hoist the resistance. The first time I put my theory into practice, I definitely felt my deltoids working like never before. I knew I was getting to a layer of fibers that had never been stressed previously. The next day my shoulders were sore in every part. I was ecstatic!

Not long after discovering this method of training, I decided to share my knowledge and, if possible, make some money with it. I wrote to Joe Weider, a well-known name in the bodybuilding field. To my surprise, Joe wrote back, asking me to elaborate on my system, which he would consider purchasing and incorporating into the Weider system of training, if it were suitable. After six years, Joe hadn't taken a position on my pre-exhaust method, so I wrote an article for *Iron Man* magazine. Peary Rader, the publisher, held the manuscript for almost two years, but eventually it appeared in 1968. My pre-exhaust method had arrived.

There was no immediate response to my training method, but soon Arthur Jones, the inventor of the Nautilus machines, was promoting the principle. He mentioned it in his Nautilus bulletin, and without actually crediting me by name, he admitted that I had invented a unique method of training. So enthused was Arthur Jones about my pre-exhaust method that he eventually incorporated it into many of his exercise machines. This was a concept that I hadn't even considered. Those machines were the backbone of Arthur Jones's enormous success and wealth.

Gradually, bodybuilders everywhere tried the pre-exhaust method, including many who had already become champions. Some dramatic prog-

ress was made, even by experienced trainers who hadn't been able to increase their muscle size for years. That's what the pre-exhaust method is all about. Bodybuilders frequently have periods when their muscle growth reaches a plateau. Some so-called hard gainers *never* get any significant muscle mass. Others enjoy plenty of initial progress, but quickly fall into the "sticking point" syndrome.

This book, like the pre-exhaust method of training, is unique. It isn't magic, but it *does* work. If you give the method a fair trial, you'll notice dramatic improvement in your muscle size. Read on. You're in for some hard training with remarkable results. It's time for some savage sets!

The legendary Joe Weider poses behind Juliette Bergman.

Mike Christian rivets the stage with his amazing "most muscular" stance.

# 1
# SETS AND REPS
## High or Low?

Whether you do one rep per workout or one hundred, you'll gain muscle, because it reacts to the physical stress placed upon it. If you work out regularly, you'll see development, regardless of the system you use to do it. I'll be the first person to admit that a number of bodybuilders had twenty-inch arms before I discovered my pre-exhaust method. Of course, today there are thousands of people with twenty-inch arms, and a portion of these bodybuilders wouldn't have built their super size without extensive use of the pre-exhaust method.

Do you want to know exactly how many sets and reps are ideal to get the job done? I could tell you to perform five sets of eight reps per body part, training on a four-day-per-week split program. However, there's no such ideal number of sets and reps that you should perform. You must tailor your routines to your *own* fitness, recuperative level, and ability to tolerate strenuous exercise. That is exactly what you must do: Adjust your training to your own personal requirements. I can only offer guidelines that have been proven to work well for many people, including beginners and champion bodybuilders, but I will always steer clear of laying down absolute law regarding the number of sets and reps to perform. The body is an ever-changing system. As certain plateaus of development and conditions are reached, training must be readjusted to promote further muscle growth.

# Beginners

Static rules are applicable only to beginners. Your first workouts are immensely important: They should neither be too hard nor too long. Basic exercises should be followed so that you're not confused with learning difficult movements. Perform eight to ten repetitions per set, except for high-rep exercises for calves, forearms, legs and abdominals.

Only one set per exercise should be performed the first week; two sets can be introduced during the second week; and three or four sets can be performed after the first month. Complete beginners shouldn't do a pre-exhaust program; it's a little too demanding and serves no special purpose at the beginning stage of bodybuilding. Use a basic routine when you start lifting weights regularly for the first time. Save the pre-exhaust method for the times when you need it most, when your muscles refuse to grow. Perform the following beginners' routine three times weekly, with at least a day's rest between each workout.

### Beginners' Routine

| | Sets | Reps |
|---|---|---|
| Standing Barbell Press | 1-3 × | 8-10 |
| Squat | 1-3 × | 10-12 |
| Bench Press | 1-3 × | 8-10 |
| Wide-grip Chin-up | 1-3 × | 8-10 |
| Barbell Curl | 1-3 × | 8-10 |
| Lying Triceps Extension | 1-3 × | 8-10 |
| Standing Calf Raise | 1-3 × | 10-15 |
| Crunch | 1-3 × | 15-20 |

Multi-joint exercises are ideal for the beginner because they work all the large muscle groups. They form the fundamental mass and size that is the basis of a good physique. However, these same basic exercises, especially when performed with low reps, can quickly lose some of their effectiveness. Bodybuilders must realize that their sport is solely concerned with appearance. Strength has little to do with the art of bodybuilding. It may look impressive to be able to toss a 400-pound barbell in the gym, but someone else may be getting better results by shape training with lighter weights, using perfect style and concentration, or by using the pre-exhaust method.

Choose the proper path early on. Remember, the shortest route is the correct routine.

## Ideal Sets and Reps

How many sets and reps? That is the question. The longer you have been training, the less noticeably you'll gain from basic low-rep training. To carve quality muscles into your physique, you will have to concentrate on higher repetitions, especially using isolation movements such as concentration curls, thigh extensions, triceps stretches, and lateral raises.

Most successful bodybuilders train using relatively high reps, twelve to fifteen, with plenty of sets, using moderate weights. Now this may seem contrary to what you've read before or what you believe to be the correct way to train. After all, we are always being told to increase the resistance if we want to get bigger muscles. Although it's true that using heavier and heavier weights is partly responsible for increasing the cellular size of muscles, more resistance leads to higher intensity. We try harder and stimulate deeper muscle cells, but we also run the risk of overtraining. Forced reps (where a partner helps you lift the weight so you can add repetitions) and negative reps (where a weight too heavy to raise is resisted strongly on its downward path) are both forms of increasing intensity that put maximum stress on your muscles, especially if low reps and heavy weights are used. But if these forms of training are not limited to one or two exercises per workout, you run the risk of overtraining your body and halting all progress.

The words "high" and "low" are, of course, relative. High reps to one bodybuilder who trains heavy may be eight; another may think that eight reps is extremely low. Let's clarify some terms about what constitutes low, medium, and high reps for bodybuilders.

## Low Reps

Five to seven reps, using about 70 to 80 percent of your maximum output for a single rep. Low reps are best suited to free-weight training. Less than five reps are normally used only by Olympic weightlifters or powerlifters, both of whom care little about development, being primarily interested in strength.

Sandra Blackie

Brad Verret curls a heavy barbell in strict form.

## Medium Reps

Eight to twelve reps. Medium reps are suited to free-weight workouts and some machines. Medium reps involve muscle hypertrophy and also stimulate capillary and mitochondria growth.

## High Reps

More than twelve reps, using good exercise form. High reps work well for advanced bodybuilders, using machines and cables, especially with the pre-exhaust, continuous tension, and iso-tension methods.

## Training Intensity

When you train using low reps and heavy weight, your muscles are apt to fail quickly. In direct contrast, those who train with lighter weights and high repetitions find that muscle failure comes slowly and painfully. The buildup of lactic acid in the muscle causes a burning sensation. How many reps should you do? Beginners need to build exercise grooves: They must learn how to balance a weight while it's being lifted. They should be able to breathe regularly during each repetition. Good form must be followed for *medium* reps during most exercises.

Intermediate bodybuilders who have been training for at least six months should by now have come to the realization that mass is built by following a varied system of repetitions. Low reps build tendon size and plump up muscle fibers. Medium reps build muscle cells and some capillary and mitochondria mass. High reps build capillary and mitochondria growth plus a small amount of cellular growth.

Experienced bodybuilders who want to gain size in the shortest time possible have three choices:

1. Train using low-rep, high-poundage exercises early in the season and high-rep, pumping-up training as a contest approaches.
2. Combine high-rep and low-rep training in the same workout.
3. Perform low-rep, heavy training on one day and follow with lighter "feeder" workouts the day after.

Britain's Bertil Fox

Lee Haney

creates confusion. Naturally, for the time factor, you should perform as few as necessary to get the job done. Beginners, as I stated earlier, have to perform only one set. As they get used to the exertion of weight training, they quickly progress to three or four sets.

Not long ago, the whole bodybuilding world was talked into performing just one or two sets per exercise by Mike Mentzer. The idea was based on the theory that *intensity* was the only facet directly related to building muscle mass. Mike openly scorned those bodybuilders who performed five or more sets of an exercise. He said that instead of performing the same thing over and over, it was far better that bodybuilders train to failure for just *one* set.

Of course, he was wrong. And the entire bodybuilding world found out the hard way. To be fair, Mike's seminars were the most interesting that I have ever heard. And his scientific theory did indeed have medical backup. What Mentzer didn't realize was that medical science had not discovered the sophisticated applications of progressive-resistance exercise, which bodybuilders had learned from over 100 years of trial-and-error training with weights.

You'll build muscle if you perform several sets per exercise. Most bodybuilders do five to eight sets per exercise. And, yes, more muscle fibers are brought into play with each successive set! This becomes even more apparent if reasonable intensity is used, and if the time between sets is limited progressively. How many sets are ideal? I recommend that you work up to five sets per exercise. If you are using supersets or pre-exhaust training, three sets are adequate.

And what about the suggested number of sets per body part? This depends on how your body responds to exercise. If you feel that a certain body area is lagging behind, you may want to raise your total sets for that area. But don't make the mistake of trying to perform that many sets for every area.

Five sets per body part is sufficient for muscle maintenance. Once you're seriously into bodybuilding, you'll need a minimum of eight sets per body part to *grow*. You may want to graduate to twelve sets for each area. Listen to your body. You'll know when you need to add more sets, and you'll know when you're performing too many. Remember that you'll benefit more by slightly undertraining than by overtraining. Stay with us!

The important point is that your overall plan involves heavy and light training. Don't lock yourself into a system that doesn't challenge your muscles over a complete and varied range of repetitions that will ultimately break down your muscle cells in such a way that they *have* to grow bigger.

The number of sets you should perform often

The monster is Gary Strydom.

Ron Love has mega-definition!

# 2
# FREQUENCY VARIATIONS
## How Often Do I Train?

"How often should I train?" I can hear you asking, but you're posing the wrong question. You should ask: "How often should I train each body part to make maximum progress?" Training frequency has to be tailored to your age, ambition, whether or not you have a physically demanding job, your diet and supplementation program, and your sleeping habits.

### Age

Young bodybuilders from fourteen to twenty-one should be concerned about overtraining. Workouts should be short and brisk; otherwise, full recuperation may not take place before the next training session. Don't train each body part more than twice a week.

Those between twenty-one and thirty enjoy the best recuperation. Ideal frequency would be to train each body part twice per week, with occasional pre-contest blitzes, lasting up to ten weeks each, of working each body area three times weekly. People over thirty, unless they have been training hard all their lives, will find a slight decrease in their recuperation ability and should probably not train each body part more than twice every seven or eight days.

## Job Demands

If your job is very demanding physically, your recuperation time may be limited. An ideal frequency for you could be the every-other-day split (described in this chapter). When you train according to this system, your workouts will be relatively short, and you'll have maximum recuperation time.

If you have a sedentary job, you may want to train according to the conventional three-days-on/one-day-off frequency, which will work each body area twice weekly (six workouts per week).

## Supplements

There's no doubt that hard-training bodybuilders can aid their recovery by taking easy-to-digest supplements between their regular meals. One-a-day-type vitamins and minerals will ob-

Shane Dimora and Ron Love compare backs.

John Terilli shows what torso development is all about.

Rick Valente and James Demelo

Lee Haney and Mike Christian strike a biceps' duo.

viously help matters if your diet is vitamin deficient. Protein powders, aminos, and glandulars are all helpful food additives that can advance your recuperation because they feed your muscles quickly and efficiently.

The most dangerous supplements are anabolic steroids, which 3 million North Americans are taking at any one time. My readers know that I am very much against steroid abuse, not just because they ultimately contribute to ill health, but because they wreck the tapered appearance of both men's and women's bodies. High dosages of steroids cause the midsection to bulge out like a barrel. It's the very opposite of what you're trying to achieve.

The old way of training, practiced almost exclusively in the fifties and sixties, was to do a total body workout three times a week. Traditionally, bodybuilders would train on Mondays, Wednesdays, and Fridays. Everything was worked—legs, back, chest, abs, shoulders, and arms—every workout day. So common was this system that many gyms were only open on these days. Of course, you don't have to base a workout around the seven-day week, but it often makes sense because of most people's work, school, and daily habits.

If you train at home, or if you are a member of a gym that is open every day of the week, you can choose your own frequency pattern, assuming that your work responsibilities don't interfere with your plans. Let's look at the different methods of training frequency.

## Every-Other-Day Split

This method is not a favorite with youngsters brimming with enthusiasm, yet it may just be the best method for them. The reason why it is disliked is because super-ambitious bodybuilders never feel that they are training often enough. Start by cutting your workout into two equal halves. Perform the first half of your workout on day one. On day two, rest completely. On day three, perform the second half of your routine. Day four is another complete rest. As you can see, this system doesn't fit into the conventional seven-day cycle. You never train two days in a row. The every-other-day split system is ideal for those who may have trouble recuperating. You are always raring to go by the

next workout. A word of caution: Your rest time between workouts is one day. Don't rest two days in a row. If this occurs, make up for the missed workout by training two days in a row. It isn't a good idea to make this a habit while training on this system.

## Four-Day Split

Like the previous system, this is very definitely an off-season method. In other words, it builds up the body, rather than reduces fat and increases muscle definition during the countdown stage before a bodybuilding contest.

This program works within the confines of the seven-day week. Split your routine into approximately two equal parts. You may do this by performing all lower-body exercises in one part, and all upper-body exercises in the other section. Alternatively, you could do the *pushing* movements (presses, triceps work, squats, etc.) one day and all the *pulling* movements (rowing, curling, chin-ups, etc.) the other day. (Actually, all muscles pull, but it *seems* like they push when you lift away from the torso.)

After dividing your workout in two parts, perform the first half on Monday, the second half on Tuesday, and rest on Wednesday. Then perform the first half again on Thursday and the second half on Friday. Rest on Saturday and Sunday. This method is ideal for married couples who want to keep their weekends free.

## Three-Days-On/One-Day-Off Routine

This system is now the most popular frequency method among serious bodybuilders. Start by dividing your workout into three parts. Each routine will be performed on a different day, three days in a row. You rest on the fourth day, then start the whole sequence again. Here's how your four-day sequence might look:

Day One: Shoulders, arms
Day Two: Legs, abdominals
Day Three: Chest, back
Day Four: Rest

Rick Valente uses an incline bench to concentrate on his curls.

Since you're only working a third of your body during each workout, you can perform more exercises, sets, and reps for each body area. Notice that your whole body is trained twice every eight days. If you feel that you're bursting with energy and enthusiasm, and that your recuperative levels are high, there is no reason why you shouldn't extend your workouts to a fourth day, taking the fifth day off as a rest.

## Six-Day Split

This method is most beneficial to those entering a contest because you actually train each body part three times a week. Begin by splitting your workout into two equal parts. Perform the first half of your routine on day one, the second half on day two. On day three, perform the first half again, then on day four, do the second part. Day five sees you working on the first half. Day six is for the second part. On day seven, take a day's rest before beginning the whole cycle again.

Progressive-overload training is very severe. Your body requires time to recover, as much as forty-eight to seventy-two hours for full recuperation. This doesn't mean that your workouts must be spaced forty-eight to seventy-two hours apart, but you should not work the same body part within that critical time frame. When you split a workout into two or three parts, you don't exercise the same muscles each day; consequently, you don't interfere with recovery time.

Sports physicians have concluded that most muscle development occurs in the so-called fast-twitch fibers. Therefore, it's vital that you stress your muscles using heavy resistance, or what your body *perceives* as heavy. This doesn't mean that you have to train for power, using five to ten sets of two to four reps with maximum weights. However, you should be conscious of trying to increase your resistance, without changing your preferred exercise style, whenever possible. A greater number of muscle fibers will be stressed when a very intense contraction occurs.

## Training Twice or Thrice Weekly

If you train your whole body three times a week, there tends to be an overlapping of muscle fatigue, because your body often fails to fully recuperate before the next workout. This fatigue compounds and eventually causes an overtrained condition and loss of muscle tissue. You may find that a few muscle areas respond well to three- or even four-times-per-week training. Calves, forearms, and abdominals are frequently cited as examples of body parts that respond to frequent training.

It's well documented that Lee Haney was in the "sticking-point doldrums" with his biceps stuck at 20½ inches. Lee increased his biceps training from twice weekly to three times weekly and it made the difference. He actually gained another one and a half inches in one year, and succeeded in building a higher biceps peak than he had ever dreamed of—no mean accomplishment for a man who had already obtained what can only be described as gigantic arms in the first place. Lee worked all his other body parts, including his triceps, twice weekly, but trained his biceps with an extra Saturday workout, consisting of five sets of dumbbell concentration curls (ten to twelve reps) and five sets of cable curls (six to eight reps). If Lee had worked every muscle group three times weekly, it is doubtful that he would have grown bigger in any area.

## No Pain, No Gain

Generally speaking, bodybuilding results are proportionate to the amount of effort that you put into your workouts. It's a fact of life that a very real pain materializes at the end of a hard set of resistance exercise. This is especially true when high-intensity effort is used for twelve, fifteen, or even twenty reps. The pre-exhaust method is well known for being painful, because two different exercises are used with only a few seconds of rest between each. This discomfort is usually localized in the muscle and is caused by fatigue acids (lactic and pyruvic). As a set progresses, these acids concentrate and irritate the nerve endings near the muscle fibers. This pain actually stimulates muscle growth.

Needless to say, not all pain is a positive sign that maximum muscle stimulation is underway. At the completion of a set, your pain should quickly disappear. If it does not, you may have pulled a muscle or injured a tendon. Joints, such as knees or shoulders, can definitely be damaged from overuse, especially where heavy weight and poor exercise style is used.

West Germany's beautiful Anja Langer

## Stretching

Stretching is an activity that everyone should get into the habit of doing. Most of the world's greatest bodybuilders stretch before their training, including multi-Olympia winners Lee Haney, Arnold Schwarzenegger, and Cory Everson. As you get older, you tend to become less flexible. Even young people lose their flexibility very quickly if they don't make a habit of stretching their muscles.

As far as the hardcore bodybuilder is con-

cerned, stretching helps prevent injury to the muscles, which in itself can save you months of lost time if you are unfortunate enough to suffer a serious injury. Stretching also strengthens your tendons and ligaments, increases your ability to work your muscles over their fullest range, and warms up and loosens them, preparing them for their regular overload training. My advice is that you stretch for a good ten minutes before each workout. I honestly believe that you'll build bigger muscles as a result.

29

Krista Anderson

# 3
# BIOLOGICAL FEEDBACK

## Listen to Your Body

You hear a great deal today about listening to your body. Competitive long-distance runners gauge exactly how far they'll run during a particular training session, depending on their body-feedback information.

Your body is updating you about its condition every waking second, but it seldom is noticed with any real sensitivity or realization that a huge amount of information is being made available to you. It's important data that can make you a more successful bodybuilder.

The most common phrases that human beings use when greeting one another invariably have to do with how we feel. "How are you?" Yet how many of us really take the trouble to think about exactly how we feel? True, our bodies don't speak to us in so many words, but nevertheless they try to communicate with us. Obvious signals, of course, are severe headaches or stomachaches, after having too much to drink or eat the previous night, or yawning when we need sleep. But there are more subtle signs that tell us other things, and if we learn our body's language, we can read the ever-present messages transmitted to our consciousness.

Bertil Fox

For example, not everyone can differentiate between fatigue and laziness, yet it's important when you learn to read the differences. If you conclude that you are genuinely tired and exhausted, working out is not a good idea. On the other hand, if you are merely listless and yawning from boredom, missing a workout is not the right answer. You will only be setting your mind and body up for a *series* of missed workouts, all of which could lead you to give up training completely.

Always be aware of how you feel. Make a mental note of it from your first waking moment. It's a good plan to keep a training log of your exercises, sets, reps, and poundages, but also include references to how you feel on a particular day. Try to analyze your different body-clock and feedback mechanisms. Your body follows a twenty-four-hour cycle known as the circadian rhythm. Your entire metabolic system undergoes changes during this period. To an extent, you program it by choosing when to sleep, when to eat, and when to train. It's wise to follow a regular pattern of living and training. In this way, your system thrives on a regular schedule. If you train every other day at five o'clock, for example, your body soon catches on, and you'll be psychologically and physiologically prepared for your alternate-day workout.

Typically, people who complete long journeys over several time zones complain of excessive fatigue, yet they also have an inability to actually sleep peacefully. Of course, their body clocks are constantly trying to reset themselves, but this always takes time. Meanwhile, they are physically and sometimes mentally disoriented. These anxieties upset both their metabolic processes and hormonal systems. As a result, their body rhythms suffer and can't get in sync, at least not enough to get 100 percent benefit from exercise programs.

Your system can only work effectively if you make an attempt to keep your body clock regular. For that reason alone, you must strive to go to bed at approximately the same time each night. Eat at regular intervals, get up at approximately the same hour, and train at about the same time of day. Obviously, this advice cannot be followed by everyone. Many people work at irregular shifts; others must grab sleep and meals whenever they can. Doctors, lawyers, factory workers, firemen, policemen, and nurses may be constantly on duty.

Magnificent Bob Paris and Mike Ashley (right).

The concentration curl is demonstrated by Yolanda Hughes.

Frequently, they can be called up at all hours. My question to these people is: "How important is your bodybuilding?" If it's the most important thing in the world, then get another job with regular hours. If your job is the most important thing, then do your best to plan your life as much as possible around your work. But don't expect to get to the top of the bodybuilding ladder.

Learn to read your body and your feedback mechanisms. Sense what is being relayed. With practice, you'll be able to obtain vital information at will. Use everything to increase your chances of developing a fitter, healthier, and more robust physique.

## Food

It doesn't take much to realize when you're hungry. Even the most simple animals know when they need food. But you should try making it a practice to eat the foods that you actually *feel* like eating. Even now your body is telling you what it wants. All you have to do is listen to it. Vince Gironda, the well-known trainer called the Iron Guru, calls this "innate animal wisdom." Does your body need carbohydrates? Is it time for red meat? Do you *feel* like eating citrus fruits?

Possibly the most obvious cravings for particular types of foods are displayed by pregnant women. Their bodies demand specific minerals or vitamins that are contained in certain foods. Bodybuilders are the same way. We can learn to recognize our food requirements. And with an improved awareness of the mind-body relationship, we can zero in and act on our precise needs at any given moment.

## Energy Levels

How do you feel right now? Most of us have some idea of how much energy we have to spend at any particular time. Of course, it's easier to recognize the extremes. There's not much doubt about our energy level when we're bubbling over with enthusiasm, ready to take on the world. Just as obvious is that drained feeling, when we feel sleepy and exhausted.

If you study your own perceptions about your energy level before a workout, you'll soon be able to tailor the intensity of your output to your

Lee Haney

Paul Jean Guillaume

energy capacity. The object is to use up your energy without draining your system completely. When you overwork your body, you're straining your whole system rather than simply stressing your muscles. You're forcing your system into a new level of stress that may throw your physiological processes into shock. This means that normal recuperation may not take place, and your muscles will cease to grow. If you're suffering from metabolic rundown, then take it easy. On the other

The ever-popular crowd-pleaser Mike Christian

hand, if your energy is at an all-time high, start pumping iron!

## Strength

Strength is, of course, related to energy, but there're times when we feel strong yet lack the energy for prolonged, high-stress workouts. Take an inventory for the truth about your strength potential before each training session. This will enable you to select not only the most suitable poundages to work out with, but you will also be in a better position to calculate the number of exercises you should perform, as well as the sets and reps for each.

Needless to say, if you feel your strength ebbing before the end of a workout, cut back on your intensity so that you can do justice to the remaining exercises. A satisfactory intensity level has to be allocated to every exercise. If you go all out on your squats and bench presses and have nothing left for your chinning and rowing exercises, your back-building aspirations will suffer. Merely going through the motions may be preferable to doing nothing at all, but it will certainly not help to develop your muscles.

## Avoiding Injuries

Bodybuilding is a very safe sport as long as you use common sense and follow a few basic rules. If you warm up correctly and perform each exercise in good style, you should be in for a lifetime of injury-free training. Injuries occur when you try to lift too much, often without a warm-up. You've heard "strength tales" about powerful men who can lift a loaded barbell or other superheavy objects *without a warm-up*. Well, these athletes are crazy. No one should attempt any kind of maximum (or near maximum) lift without a proper warm-up.

About three times a year, a former Mr. America used to drop into a gym where I trained. He was usually accompanied by his latest girlfriend, and always claimed that he hadn't managed to find time to train. His usual routine was to talk to the gym owner for a few minutes, then he would load up a barbell to about 350 pounds. Without even taking off his jacket, he would bench press the weight once or twice. He was proudest of the fact that he still could bench press such a heavy weight "cold," giving the impression that if he warmed up, he could lift far more. The last time he visited the gym, his left pectoral muscle suffered a massive tear and this former Mr. America hasn't been seen since.

Observe the following simple rules and you'll avoid injuries.

*Warm up for every exercise with at least one set of twelve to fifteen reps using a moderate weight.* Excessively light weights do not warm up your muscles. Heavy exercises like squats, bench presses, and deadlifts require several warm-up sets; add weight with each successive set.

*Don't perform any ballistic movements.* Never bounce out of a squat. Refrain from hitting the bar on your sternum in the bench press. Never jerk your body in the bent-over rowing exercise. Extend your arms slowly and smoothly into the straight-arm position in the preacher curl.

*Never allow your ego to control your workouts.* Many injuries occur as a result of bodybuilders attempting to lift too much in order to impress other gym members or friends.

*Perform a few basic stretches at the beginning of every workout.* Hold each stretch for ten to fifteen seconds. The resulting improvement in ligament and tendon strength and flexibility will help guard against injury.

Never eat a big meal before working out. It will drain you of energy. If you must eat before training, have a small snack or a light sandwich and head for the gym. It can be hard to distinguish between feeling laziness and genuine fatigue. You may find it easier if you evaluate your activity of the previous two days. Did you do anything out of the ordinary in your workouts, such as performing many more sets of squats or running double your usual distance? Fatigue usually has a very real foundation. Laziness, on the other hand, can result from boredom, overeating, or general lack of enthusiasm and motivation. A truly inspired bodybuilder seldom suffers from laziness in any form. If you are truly fatigued, you should miss your workout completely. If you suspect that you're only suffering from laziness, then start working out and your enthusiasm and desire to train should return after the first half-dozen sets.

Don't underestimate your ultimate power to read your body's feedback system. Learn the language and become a better physical culturist!

Britain's top honcho Frank Richards

Brian Homka uses the Nautilus pullover machine with the help of training partner Scott Wilson.

# 4
# TIME TO TRAIN
## Pre-Exhaust Routines

Because the number of pure isolation exercises is limited, there aren't huge numbers of pre-exhaust variations. Even though I invented the pre-exhaust system, I have never claimed that it's the *only* worthwhile system of training. I do say with utter conviction that it's a workable method that's worth trying even when everything else fails. It worked for me and for many name bodybuilders who have tried it extensively. Some, like Mike Mentzer, used it exclusively when attempting to add muscle mass for bodybuilding competitions.

You don't have to make an entire routine of pre-exhaust combinations. There's no reason in the world why you shouldn't perform straight sets for most of your body parts and just use the pre-exhaust method for one or two muscle groups that need special attention. Remember, when you use the pre-exhaust system, you're using one of the most intense methods known. Your body may not be suited to a full-fledged pre-exhaust routine for every body area.

People vary in their capacity to endure heavy physical stress. Their natural tolerance for strenuous exercise is low. For this reason, everyone who embarks on a formal exercise system or new diet plan should consult with his or her doctor. This is most important if you're over forty or have a his-

Yolanda Hughes performs the triceps extension.

best to err on the side of caution.

When you begin a brand-new routine, whether it involves the pre-exhaust method or not, I suggest that you never go the limit in your physical effort. New exercises or different combinations can work your muscles from new angles and minor tears or strains could occur. This is especially true in cases when you perform a progressive-resistance exercise that you have never done before. Remember, you are "cutting" a new groove in your muscles. It takes at least a couple of workouts for your body to get accustomed to it. After three workouts or so, you are ready to blitz your muscles to your heart's content.

The essence of pre-exhaust training, as I explained earlier, is to tire out or temporarily exhaust a particular muscle, and then to *immediately* involve this same muscle in a combination movement where it has become the weakest link. During the combination, multi-joint exercise, this muscle now has to work especially hard to keep the movement going. More fibers are forced to contract, which translates into additional muscle growth.

As you may know, the triceps are the weak links involved in many chest exercises. In other words, when you do dips, bench presses, or incline presses, the triceps are worked hard and the pectorals only moderately. This means that your triceps may well grow more rapidly than your chest. That's fine if you already have a large chest, but if you want to develop those pecs, nothing will do it quite as fast as the pre-exhaust system.

The way to get around the weak-link triceps is to isolate the pecs first with an exercise like cable crossovers, or dumbbell flyes, or pec-deck flyes, where the triceps are not directly involved. After a hard set, performing the exercises to the point of failure, proceed immediately to the combination exercise, such as incline or bench presses. Your triceps will be temporarily stronger than your pectorals, which will be in a state of near exhaustion. This forces your pectorals to take on extra effort. One of the biggest complaints among bodybuilders is that even though they train a specific muscle, they can't really "feel it." My pre-exhaust method will virtually guarantee that you'll feel it. And what's more, you'll grow from it, too!

The following routine is a complete pre-exhaust workout involving just one exercise combination (two exercises) per body part. The sets and reps listed are just for your guidance. Begin-

tory of heart, circulatory, or other physiological problems. It's far better to check first and be sure than to not have a physical checkup and collapse in the middle of a workout. Chances are, your doctor will whole-heartedly recommend that you perform a regular exercise program, but it's always

Negrita Jayde works her thigh biceps with a standing leg curl.

ners should only perform one set; advanced body-builders may want to perform four or five sets.

It's vital that you don't rest between the isolation and combination movement. Interestingly, even fifteen or twenty seconds of rest will bring about an 80 percent rate of recovery. Those trainers new to the pre-exhaust method, though not complete beginners to training, should perform two sets, using moderate poundage for the first couple of workouts. As you get used to this technique, you can work out with maximum poundages and increase the number of sets.

43

### Pre-Exhaust Routine

| Shoulders | | Sets | | Reps |
|---|---|---|---|---|
| Dumbbell Lateral Raise | } Alternate | 3 | × | 12 |
| Press Behind Neck | | 3 | × | 8 |

| Chest | | | | |
|---|---|---|---|---|
| Flat Bench Flye | } Alternate | 3 | × | 10 |
| Bench Press | | 3 | × | 8 |

| Thighs | | | | |
|---|---|---|---|---|
| Thigh Extension | } Alternate | 3 | × | 12 |
| Back Squat | | 3 | × | 10 |

| Back | | | | |
|---|---|---|---|---|
| Bent-arm Pullover | } Alternate | 3 | × | 15 |
| T-bar Row | | 3 | × | 10 |

| Abdominals | | | | |
|---|---|---|---|---|
| Crunch | } Alternate | 3 | × | 15 |
| Hanging Knee Raise | | 3 | × | 20 |

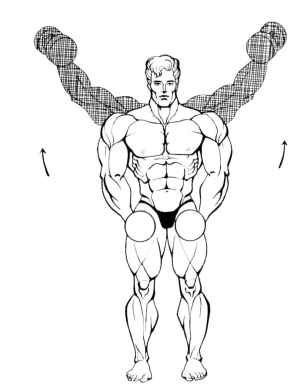

Dumbbell Lateral Raise

Press Behind Neck

44

Back Squat

Thigh Extension

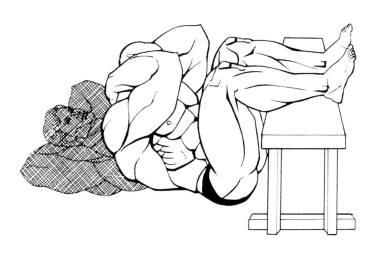

Crunch

Hanging Knee Raise

45

| Calves | | Sets | Reps |
|---|---|---|---|
| Standing Calf Raise | } Alternate | 3 × | 25 |
| Rope Jumping (weighted handles) | | 3 × | 3 min. |

| Biceps | | | |
|---|---|---|---|
| Preacher Bench Dumbbell Curl (90°) | } Alternate | 3 × | 12 |
| Under-grip Chin-up | | 3 × | 10-15 |

| Triceps | | | |
|---|---|---|---|
| Triceps Pressdown (lat machine) | } Alternate | 3 × | 12 |
| Close-grip Bench Press | | 3 × | 12 |

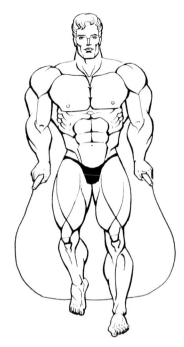

Rope Jumping

Standing Calf Raise

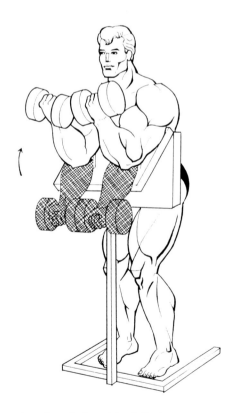

Preacher Bench Dumbbell Curl

46

Under-grip Chin-up

Triceps Pressdown

Close-grip Barbell Bench Press

*Forearms*
| | | | |
|---|---|---|---|
| Reverse Wrist Curl | } Alternate | 3 × | 12 |
| Reverse Curl | | 3 × | 15 |

The following exercises can be used for pre-exhaust training:

*Thighs*
*Isolation Movements*
Thigh Extension, Roman Chair Squat
*Combination Movements*
Back Squat, Front Squat, Hack Slide, Barbell Hack Lift

*Middle Chest*
*Isolation Movements*
Flat Bench Flye, Cable Crossover, Pec-Deck Flye
*Combination Movements*
Supine Bench Press, Dumbbell Bench Press

*Upper Chest*
*Isolation Movement*
Incline Bench Flye (dumbbells or cables) (40-45°)
*Combination Movements*
Incline Bench Press, Incline Bench Dumbbell Press

Reverse Wrist Curl

Reverse Curl

Incline Bench Dumbbell Flye

Incline Bench Press

*Lower Chest*
*Isolation Movements*
Decline Bench Flye, Decline Bench Cable Cross-over
*Combination Movements*
Wide-grip Parallel Bar Dip, Decline Bench Press, Decline Bench Dumbbell Press


*Thigh Biceps*
*Isolation Movements*
Supine Leg Curl (machine), Standing Leg Curl
*Combination Movements*
Upside-down Squat (gravity boots)

*Waist*
*Isolation Movements*
Crunch
*Combination Movements*
Hanging Leg Raise, Inverted Sit-up (gravity boots)


*Back*
*Isolation Movements*
Nautilus Pullover, Barbell Pullover, Parallel Bar Shrug
*Combination Movements*
Bent-over Row, Chin-up to Chest, T-bar Row

*Trapezius*
*Isolation Movements*
Shrugs (dumbbells, barbell, calf machine, Universal machine)
*Combination Movements*
Upright Row, Smith Machine Clean

*Biceps*
*Isolation Movements*
Preacher Bench Curl (dumbbells or barbell) (90°)
*Combination Movements*
Narrow-undergrip Chin-up

*Triceps*
*Isolation Movements*
Cable Pressdown, Standing Barbell Extension, Lying Triceps Stretch to Forehead
*Combination Movements*
Narrow-grip Bench Press, Parallel Bar Dip

*Front Shoulders*
*Isolation Movements*
Alternate Dumbbell Front Raise, Barbell Front Raise, Simultaneous Dumbbell Front Raise
*Combination Movements*
Incline Bench Barbell Press (80°), Dumbbell Bench Press

*Rear Shoulders*
*Isolation Movements*
Bent-over Dumbbell Flye, Bent-over Cable Flye, Pec-Deck (reverse position), Rear Delt Machine
*Combination Movements*
Bent-over Barbell Row, Seated Cable Row, Behind-Back Row

*Side Shoulders*
*Isolation Movements*
Lateral Raise, Cable Side Raise, Machine Lateral Raise
*Combination Movements*
Wide-grip Upright Row, Press Behind Neck

*Forearms*
*Isolation Movement*
Reverse Wrist Curl
*Combination Movement*
Reverse Curl

*Calves*
*Isolation Movements*
Toe Raise (leg-press machine), Standing Calf Raise, Donkey Calf Raise (45°), Machine Toe Raise
*Combination Movements*
Rope Jumping, High Rebounder Jump

Parallel Bar Shrug

Bent-over Row

Check out the perfect form in Paul Jean Guillaume's preacher bench curl.
See over for the full photographic sequence.

## Pre-Exhaust Strength Training

The pre-exhaust system has been used with some success by powerlifters to increase their strength. After all, the method does strengthen your weaker body areas. As the inventor of the pre-exhaust method, it might be an attractive ego boost to claim that powerlifters would be automatically able to double their weight totals if they used the pre-exhaust system, but that would be an exaggeration.

Heavy-duty ambassador Mike Mentzer built his thigh strength so that he could squat with 600 pounds using the pre-exhaust system, alternating thigh extensions with back squats. He also developed his chest power to the extent of being able to bench press 500 pounds, alternating flyes with regular bench presses.

Powerlifters usually perform six to ten straight sets of two to five reps, taking plenty of rest between exercises and sets. This is probably the best way to build pure strength for powerlifting.

#2

#3

#4

#5

#6

#7

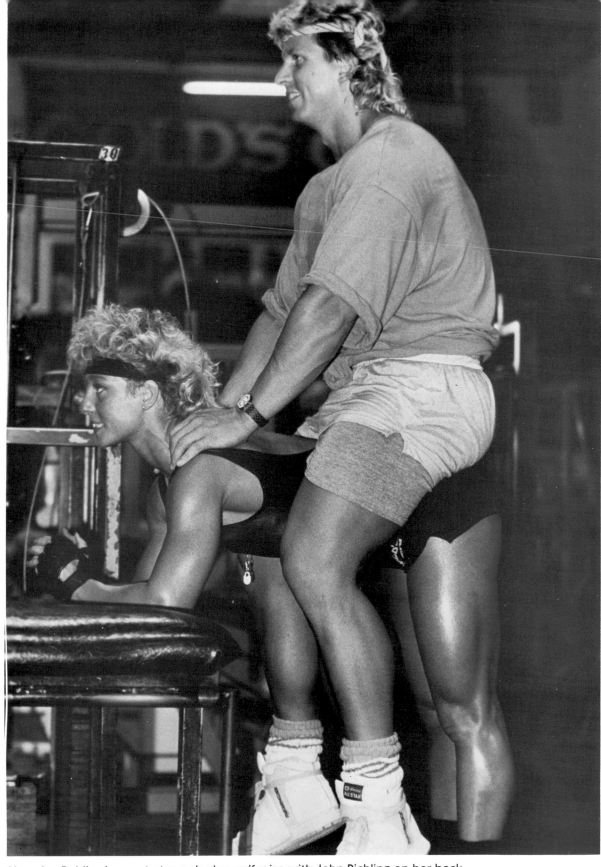

Veronica Dahlin demonstrates a donkey calf raise with John Richling on her back.

# 5
# PRE-EXHAUST SPECIALIZATION
## Routines for Specific Results

As I have indicated previously, you don't have to use the pre-exhaust method for every body part; indeed, this may be too severe for your body's recuperation process to handle. My original reason for inventing this method was to create a massive blitz situation that literally forced the target muscles to grow. Initially, I had not anticipated using the pre-exhaust method for every muscle and every workout. I believe it was Mr. Universe Mike Mentzer who first advocated this in his "heavy-duty seminars," which were arguably the most scientific lessons in bodybuilding ever made.

Straight sets, performing one set of a particular exercise after another until approximately three to five sets have been completed, is a very good method of training. Every male and female bodybuilding champion has used this method. And more importantly, they have achieved a lot of muscle mass from the practice. The following is a workable straight-sets routine that is typical of the type used by ambitious bodybuilders of both sexes.

## Straight-Sets Routine

*Shoulders*
Seated Press Behind Neck
Upright Row
Lateral Raise
Bent-over Flye

*Thighs*
Front Squat (heels on 2″ block)
Hack Lift
Thigh Curl

*Chest*
Wide-grip Bench Press to Upper Sternum
Incline Bench Dumbbell Press (40°)
Incline Bench Dumbbell Flye (35°)

*Back*
Prone Hyperextension
Wide-grip Chin Behind Neck
Single-arm Dumbbell Row

*Calves*
Standing Calf Raise
Donkey Calf Raise

*Trapezius*
Dumbbell Shrug

*Abdominals*
Hanging Leg Raise
Crunch
Broomstick Twist

*Forearms*
Seated Wrist Curl (barbell)
Reverse Curl

*Biceps*
Cheating Barbell Curl
Incline Dumbbell Curl (45°)
Supine Dumbbell Curl (high bench)

*Triceps*
Lying Triceps Stretch
E-Z Bar Triceps Stretch (holding center of bar)
Reverse Bench Dip

Vaughn Jipner wraps his knees before he attempts some super-heavy 45-degree leg presses (opposite).

## Pre-Exhaust Chest Routines

### Upper Chest Routine One

| | | Sets | | Reps |
|---|---|---|---|---|
| Incline Bench Dumbbell Flye | Alternate | 4 | × | 12 |
| Incline Bench Barbell Press | | 4 | × | 10 |

### Upper Chest Routine Two

| | | | | |
|---|---|---|---|---|
| Incline Bench Cable Flye | Alternate | 4 | × | 15 |
| Incline Bench Dumbbell Press | | 4 | × | 12 |

### Upper Chest Routine Three

| | | | | |
|---|---|---|---|---|
| Cable Crossover (chin-level hands) | Alternate | 4 | × | 12 |
| Incline Barbell Bench Press (wide grip) | | 4 | × | 12 |

### Middle Chest Routine One

| | | | | |
|---|---|---|---|---|
| Flat Bench Cable Flye | Alternate | 4 | × | 15 |
| Flat Bench Dumbbell Press | | 4 | × | 12 |

### Middle Chest Routine Two

| | | | | |
|---|---|---|---|---|
| Flat Bench Dumbbell Flye | Alternate | 3 | × | 12 |
| Barbell Bench Press | | 3 | × | 10 |

### Middle Chest Routine Three

| | | | | |
|---|---|---|---|---|
| Cable Crossover (chest-level hands) | Alternate | 3 | × | 12 |
| Flat Bench Dumbbell Press | | 3 | × | 12 |

### Middle Chest Routine Four

| | | | | |
|---|---|---|---|---|
| Pec-Deck Flye | Alternate | 3 | × | 15 |
| Vertical Bench Press Machine | | 3 | × | 12 |

### Middle Chest Routine Five

| | | | | |
|---|---|---|---|---|
| Flat Bench Dumbbell Flye | Alternate | 3 | × | 12 |
| Universal Machine Bench Press | | 3 | × | 10 |

### Lower Chest Routine One

| | | | | |
|---|---|---|---|---|
| Decline Bench Cable Flye | Alternate | 3 | × | 12 |
| Decline Bench Barbell Press | | 3 | × | 12 |

### Lower Chest Routine Two

| | | | | |
|---|---|---|---|---|
| Decline Bench Dumbbell Flye | Alternate | 4 | × | 12 |
| Decline Bench Dumbbell Press | | 4 | × | 10 |

### Lower Chest Routine Three

| | | | | |
|---|---|---|---|---|
| Cable Crossover (waist-level hands) | Alternate | 3 | × | 15 |
| Decline Bench Barbell Press | | 3 | × | 12 |

### Lower Chest Routine Four

| | | | | |
|---|---|---|---|---|
| Decline Bench Dumbbell Flye | Alternate | 3 | × | 20 |
| Parallel Bar Dip | | 3 | × | 15 |

### Outer Chest Routine One

| | | | | |
|---|---|---|---|---|
| Cable Crossover | Alternate | 4 | × | 15 |
| Wide-grip Barbell Bench Press | | 4 | × | 12 |

### Outer Chest Routine Two

| | | | | |
|---|---|---|---|---|
| Flat Bench Dumbbell Flye | Alternate | 4 | × | 15 |
| Wide-grip Parallel Bar Dip | | 4 | × | 15 |

### Inner Chest Routine One

| | | | | |
|---|---|---|---|---|
| Cable Crossover | Alternate | 3 | × | 15 |
| Shoulder-width Barbell Bench Press | | 3 | × | 10 |

### Inner Chest Routine Two

| | | | | |
|---|---|---|---|---|
| Pec-Deck Flye | Alternate | 3 | × | 15 |
| Shoulder-width Incline Barbell Bench Press (35°) | | 3 | × | 12 |

## Pre-Exhaust Trapezius Routines

### Trapezius Routine One

| | | | | |
|---|---|---|---|---|
| Dumbbell Shrug | Alternate | 3 | × | 15 |
| Barbell Clean | | 3 | × | 12 |

### Trapezius Routine Two

| | | | | |
|---|---|---|---|---|
| Barbell Shrug | Alternate | 3 | × | 12 |
| Upright Row (close grip) | | 3 | × | 10-12 |

### Trapezius Routine Three

| | | | | |
|---|---|---|---|---|
| Universal Machine Shrug | | 4 | × | 12 |
| Smith Machine Clean (shoulder width grip) | | 4 | × | 12 |

California's Brad Verret squeezes out a cable crossover for his chest.

## Pre-Exhaust Back Routines

### Upper Back Routine One

| Barbell Pullover | } Alternate | 3 × 12 |
| Chin-up to Chest | | 3 × 12 |

### Upper Back Routine Two

| Parallel Bar Shrug | } Alternate | 3 × 15-20 |
| Wide-grip Chin-up Behind Neck | | 3 × 10-12 |

### Middle Back Routine One

| Nautilus Pullover | } Alternate | 3 × 15 |
| T-bar Row | | 3 × 15 |

### Middle Back Routine Two

| Bent-arm Barbell Pullover | } Alternate | 4 × 12 |
| Bent-over Row | | 4 × 10 |

## Pre-Exhaust Biceps Routines

### Biceps Routine One

| | | Sets | Reps |
| Dumbbell Preacher Curl (90°) | } Alternate | 3 × | 10 |
| Close-undergrip Chin | | 3 × | 10-15 |

### Biceps Routine Two

| Barbell Preacher Curl (90°) | } Alternate | 3 × | 10 |
| Close-undergrip Chin | | 3 × | 10-15 |

### Biceps Routine Three

| Bent-over Barbell Concentration Curl | } Alternate | 4 × | 12 |
| Cheating Barbell Curl | | 4 × | 12 |

## Pre-Exhaust Thigh Routines

| Middle Thigh Routine | | Sets | | Reps |
|---|---|---|---|---|
| Leg Extension | Alternate | 4 | × | 15 |
| Front Squat | | 4 | × | 12 |

| Upper Thigh Routine | | Sets | | Reps |
|---|---|---|---|---|
| Leg Extension (supine bench) | Alternate | 3 | × | 15 |
| Back Squat (feet flat) | | 3 | × | 12 |

| Lower Thigh Routine | | Sets | | Reps |
|---|---|---|---|---|
| Roman-Chair Squat | Alternate | 4 | × | 20 |
| Hack Squat (barbell) | | 4 | × | 20 |

## Pre-Exhaust Waist Routines

| Lower Waist Routine | | Sets | | Reps |
|---|---|---|---|---|
| Bench Knee Raise | Alternate | 4 | × | 20 |
| Horizontal Bar Leg Raise | | 4 | × | 15 |

| Middle and Upper Waist Routine One | | Sets | | Reps |
|---|---|---|---|---|
| Crunch | Alternate | 3 | × | 15 |
| Horizontal Bar Knee Raise | | 3 | × | 15 |

| Middle and Upper Waist Routine Two | | Sets | | Reps |
|---|---|---|---|---|
| Lying Bench Crunch | Alternate | 3 | × | 15 |
| Inverted Sit-up (gravity boots) | | 3 | × | 12 |

## Pre-Exhaust Thigh Biceps Routines

| Thigh Biceps Routine One | | Sets | | Reps |
|---|---|---|---|---|
| Lying Leg Curl | Alternate | 4 | × | 15 |
| Upside-down Squat (gravity boots) | | 4 | × | 10-12 |

| Thigh Biceps Routine Two | | Sets | | Reps |
|---|---|---|---|---|
| Standing Leg Curl | Alternate | 4 | × | 12 |
| Face-down Body Curl | | 4 | × | 15 |

## Pre-Exhaust Forearm Routines

| Forearm Routine One | | Sets | | Reps |
|---|---|---|---|---|
| Reverse Wrist Curl | Alternate | 4 | × | 15 |
| Reverse Curl | | 4 | × | 15-20 |

| Forearm Routine Two | | Sets | | Reps |
|---|---|---|---|---|
| Wrist Curl | Alternate | 4 | × | 25 |
| Close-grip Partial Pulldown | | 4 | × | 20 |

Lee Haney shows how he performs a thigh extension at a training session.

Anita Gandol pre-exhausts her front deltoid with a cable forward raise.

An excellent triceps isolation exercise demonstrated with a cable by Paul Jean Guillaume.

## Pre-Exhaust Triceps Routines

| *Triceps Outer Head Routine* | | Sets | | Reps |
|---|---|---|---|---|
| Face-down Cradle Bench Extension | Alternate | 4 | × | 15 |
| Close-grip Bench Press (elbows out) | | 4 | × | 12 |

| *Lower Triceps Routine* | | | | |
|---|---|---|---|---|
| Single-dumbbell Behind Head Extension | Alternate | 4 | × | 15 |
| Parallel Bar Dip | | 4 | × | 15 |

| *Triceps Belly Routine One* | | | | |
|---|---|---|---|---|
| Triceps Pressdown | Alternate | 4 | × | 12-15 |
| Narrow-grip Bench Press (elbows in) | | 4 | × | 12 |

| *Triceps Belly Routine Two* | | | | |
|---|---|---|---|---|
| Lying Barbell Stretch to Forehead | Alternate | 4 | × | 12 |
| Parallel Bar Dip (elbows in) | | 4 | × | 12-15 |

| *Triceps Belly Routine Three* | | | | |
|---|---|---|---|---|
| Seated Triceps Barbell Stretch (elbows in) | Alternate | 4 | × | 10-12 |
| Close-grip Bench Press (elbows in) | | 4 | × | 12 |

The triceps pressdown—Sven Ole Thorsen shows how.

Veronica Dahlin performs a standing dumbbell press with ideal form. (Here and opposite.)

## Pre-Exhaust Shoulder Routines

| | | Sets | | Reps |
|---|---|---|---|---|
| *Rear Shoulder Routine One* | | | | |
| Bent-over Dumbbell Flye | } Alternate | 3 | × | 12-15 |
| T-bar Row (elbows out) | | 3 | × | 15 |
| *Rear Shoulder Routine Two* | | | | |
| Bent-over Cable Flye | } Alternate | 3 | × | 15 |
| Seated Pulley Row (elbows out) | | 3 | × | 15 |
| *Rear Shoulder Routine Three* | | | | |
| Rear-Delt Machine Flye | } Alternate | 3 | × | 15 |
| High Bench Face-down Row | | 3 | × | 12-15 |
| *Front Shoulder Routine One* | | | | |
| Alternate Dumbbell Forward Raise | } Alternate | 3 | × | 12 |
| Dumbbell Bench Press | | 3 | × | 15 |
| *Front Shoulder Routine Two* | | | | |
| Incline Bench Barbell Forward Raise | } Alternate | 3 | × | 12-15 |
| Wide-grip Barbell Bench Press | | 3 | × | 12-15 |
| *Front Shoulder Routine Three* | | | | |
| Face-down Forward Dumbbell Raise | } Alternate | 3 | × | 12 |
| Incline Barbell Bench Press (45°) | | 3 | × | 10-12 |
| *Side Deltoid Routine One* | | | | |
| Lateral Raise | } Alternate | 3 | × | 12 |
| Wide-grip Upright Row | | 3 | × | 12 |
| *Side Deltoid Routine Two* | | | | |
| Cable Side Raise | } Alternate | 3 | × | 12-15 |
| Military Press (elbows out) | | 3 | × | 12 |
| *Side Deltoid Routine Three* | | | | |
| Lateral Raise | } Alternate | 3 | × | 10 |
| Seated Press Behind Neck | | 3 | × | 12 |
| *Side Deltoid Routine Four* | | | | |
| Machine Lateral Raise | } Alternate | 3 | × | 12-15 |
| Press Behind Neck (squat racks) | | 3 | × | 8 |

## Pre-Exhaust Calf Routines

| | | Sets | | Reps |
|---|---|---|---|---|
| *Calf Routine One* | | | | |
| Toe Raise (leg-press machine) | } Alternate | 3 | × | 20 |
| Rope Jumping | | 3 | × | 2 min. |
| *Calf Routine Two* | | | | |
| Donkey Calf Raise | } Alternate | 3 | × | 15-20 |
| Trampoline or Rebounder | | 3 | × | 3 min. |

*Side Deltoid Routine Five*

| Lateral Raise (strands) | | 3 × 12 |
|---|---|---|
| Smith Machine or Universal Machine Press | Alternate | 3 × 10 |

This concludes our specialization routines for the pre-exhaust method. If you think up new variations, then use them by all means. If you have any problems, I can always be reached via my office at *MuscleMag International*, 2 Melanie Drive, Unit 7, Brampton, Ontario, Canada L6T 4K8.

Phil Hill and Bob Paris (right) pose off at the IFBB New York Night of Champions.

# 6
# THE COMPLETE PROGRAM
## "Do It This Way"

One of the advantages of the pre-exhaust method—incidentally, an aspect that I didn't even consider when I invented it—is that if it's performed efficiently and with single-minded purpose, it saves you considerable time in accomplishing your goal of developing your body.

When you are young and enthusiastic, you can always find time to train. Why? Because building your muscles is often a top priority. As you get older, more and more things take your free moments away from you. Work, family, children, and countless other duties can leave you with little time for personal hobbies. At the time when I invented the pre-exhaust system, I couldn't have cared less about saving time. I would have found six hours a day to train if I thought it would have helped me get bigger muscles.

Nevertheless, as luck would have it, the pre-exhaust method not only turned out to be extremely workable as a muscle-building system, but it's also the most time-efficient method yet devised, even more so than the conventional supersets method. Many bodybuilders who are short of time adopt the supersets system of training simply because performing sets of exercises in pairs, with virtually no rest time in between, saves several hours each week. Now the pre-exhaust method saves even more time because the severity of the exercise enables you to fully stimulate your muscles using fewer sets per body part.

Usually, when I write about bodybuilding, I make general statements and offer several suggestions about training, leaving the actual compilation of your workout and the specifics of your training frequency for you to design. However, a considerable number of individuals have complaints, saying that they want to be told exactly what to do—how to train, how often to exercise, what to eat, etc. Perhaps this is why the *one-on-one* coaching system is so popular. People don't want to be bothered with working things out for themselves.

Recently, a woman asked me for training advice. She had read *Pumping Up!* and *Superpump!*, two books that I had co-authored with IFBB (International Federation of Bodybuilders) president, Ben Weider. This woman was convinced that I was the only person in the world who could offer her the kind of help she was seeking. She wanted me to be her personal trainer. I told her that *Superpump!* contained a perfect beginner's routine, that many thousands of women were using it successfully, training two or three times a week. I explained that if I trained her, I would give her that very same basic routine. I would also put her on a diet that appeared in the book. Even though I mentioned that running the day-to-day business of *MuscleMag International*, my bodybuilding magazine, took much of my time, she asked me to train her for four workouts a week.

Rich Gaspari gives some pointers on exercise form at a recent seminar.

Backs don't get much wider than this! John Terilli illustrates a lat spread.

Yolanda Hughes works her shoulders with the upright row combination movement.

While I enjoy making money, I'm very much against getting it by taking advantage of others. With this lady, I had a dilemma. I value my own time at around $500 an hour, yet I knew that I couldn't in all conscience charge her that amount to put her through a workout. I told her all this, and to my surprise she still wanted me to train her at the cost of $2,000 a week! The truth is, I trained her for one workout at no charge, then told her that I just didn't have the time to train her or anyone else

exclusively. Incidentally, the last time I went to the gym, I saw her with a personal trainer!

It's often true that people want to be told *exactly* what to do and when to do it. For that reason, I have decided to include this Chapter. There are no gray areas. If you have your own ideas of how to arrange your eating habits, training, and supplementation, then skip over the rest of this Chapter. For those of you who want to take orders, read and adopt these rules.

70

Gunter Kuhni pauses on the incline bench.

John Hnatyshack

## Training Frequency

Train four days a week—preferably Mondays, Tuesdays, Thursdays, and Fridays. Don't train more than two days in a row. Begin by dividing your routine into two equal parts. Perform the first half of your workout on Monday and the second half on Tuesday. Rest completely on Wednesday. Then perform the first half of your workout again on Thursday and the second half on Friday. Your weekend is free for social or family obligations.

## The Workout

Perform every movement in strict exercise style. Don't bounce, heave, or cheat the weight up or down. Complete every rep with controlled deliberation. The first set of every exercise should act as a warm-up. Use only a moderate weight resistance. Subsequent sets can be performed with more intensity, but always make sure that your muscles are warmed up adequately before using maximum effort. Follow the rules for pre-exhaust training to the letter in Chapter 4.

If you are a beginner to bodybuilding, you *must* start with very low weight. Perform one set only per exercise until you have conditioned your body so that you can add weight and increase intensity.

## Rest and Relaxation

Sleep eight hours every night. If this proves to be impossible, make sure that you are in bed for that period of time whether or not you actually sleep. Lying supine, even though you may not be sleeping, can help your body recover from exercise and fully recuperate for the following day. Relax for twenty minutes after each meal with your feet up. Never perform vigorous physical activity immediately after eating. Your stomach needs additional blood supplies to aid digestion, and strenuous activity can re-direct those supplies to other areas.

### The Pre-Exhaust Routine
Remember to alternate the performance of the exercise pairs for each body part in the routine. For instance, perform one set of seated presses

Marjo Selin (left) performs a triceps pressdown as training partner Tonya Knight observes.

behind neck, followed by one set of standing lateral raises for your shoulders. Repeat the alternating sequence for three sets.

| Shoulders | | Sets | | Reps |
|---|---|---|---|---|
| Seated Press Behind Neck | Alternate | 3 | × | 12 |
| Standing Lateral Raise | | 3 | × | 15 |

| Thighs | | | | |
|---|---|---|---|---|
| Thigh Extensions | Alternate | 3 | × | 12 |
| Squats | | 3 | × | 15 |

| Chest | | | | |
|---|---|---|---|---|
| Incline Dumbbell Flye | Alternate | 3 | × | 12 |
| Incline Barbell French Press | | 3 | × | 10 |

| Back | | | | |
|---|---|---|---|---|
| Parallel Bar Shrug | Alternate | 3 | × | 15 |
| Bent-over Barbell Rowing | | 3 | × | 12 |

| Abdominals | | | | |
|---|---|---|---|---|
| Crunch | Alternate | 3 | × | 15 |
| Hanging Knee Raise | | 3 | × | 20 |

| Forearms | | | | |
|---|---|---|---|---|
| Seated Reverse Wrist Curl | Alternate | 3 | × | 12 |
| Standing Reverse Curl | | 3 | × | 12 |

| Calves | | | | |
|---|---|---|---|---|
| Standing Calf Raise | Alternate | 3 | × | 20 |
| Rope Jumping | | 3 | × | 2 min. |

| Biceps | | | | |
|---|---|---|---|---|
| Preacher Bench Dumbbell Curl | Alternate | 3 | × | 10 |
| Under-grip Chin-up | | 3 | × | 12 |

| Triceps | | | | |
|---|---|---|---|---|
| Triceps Pressdown | Alternate | 3 | × | 12 |
| Close-Grip Barbell Bench Press | | 3 | × | 15 |

## Nutrition

Your only concern regarding nutrition should be that you eat as healthily as you possibly can. Eat only fresh, natural, unprocessed foods to ensure that your muscles are supplied with the best-quality nutrients available. Don't consume superfluous, empty calories that will only develop fat on your body. We all need different amounts so you will have to be your own director of quantities. Read the complete section on nutrition in Chapter 8. Here are some nutritionally sound diet suggestions:

*Breakfast*
Muesli or bran cereal with chopped fruit (apples, bananas, blueberries, or strawberries)
Boiled or poached eggs
Skim or low-fat milk
*Mid-Morning Snack*
Fresh fruits or vegetables
Skim or low-fat milk
*Lunch*
Cold turkey or tuna fish
Tossed salad (lettuce, cucumbers, tomatoes, onions)
Whole-grain bread
Fresh fruit (apples, apricots, plums, melon)
*Mid-Afternoon Snack*
Fat-free yogurt or cottage cheese
*Dinner*
Broiled chicken or fish
Baked potato
Steamed mixed vegetables (cauliflower, broccoli, carrots, green beans)
Baked apple
*Evening Snack*
Skim or low-fat milk
Bran muffin

## Supplementation

Eat well and you don't need supplements. That's a pretty fair statement for people who are not involved in regular strenuous exercise. I firmly believe that vitamin and mineral supplements are worthwhile investments. You should rest assured that you're getting all the essential nutrients when you supplement your diet correctly. If you want to gain weight, make a habit of drinking two glasses of milk and egg protein (mixed with 2 percent milk) per day between meals. For those of you who don't wish to gain weight, supplement your diet with free-form amino acids. All regular weight trainers should take a daily vitamin/mineral pack.

The remarkable biceps of John Terilli during some concentration curling.

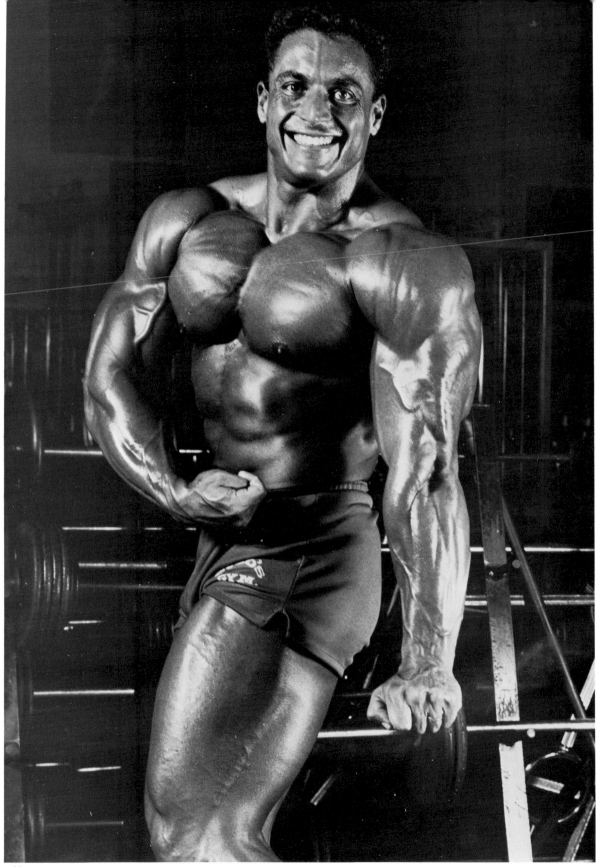

Harry Dodich

# 7
# HIGH-REP TRAINING
## Promoting Weight Loss

People often find it hard to believe that weight training can both increase muscle and decrease weight, but it's true. By tailoring your sets and reps to burn more calories, and by reducing calories in your diet, you can cause weight loss to take place. Anyone really involved in the bodybuilding way of life knows that a five-or ten pound loss in a week is not impossible. However, it's probably best to lose weight comparatively slowly at two or three pounds a week. You don't want to shock your system too quickly or drastically.

Your first task is to mentally define what you want to look like. Are you currently overweight, or are you merely carrying a surface layer of fat under your skin that hides your muscles? Some people even feel that they are too muscular in certain areas. This, too, can be reduced by diet and exercise. It's no harder to remove muscle than fat; you just have to follow the rules diligently. Few people, however, are in a position where they want to reduce muscle size, but the problem does exist for some.

Renee Casella (left), Janice Graser (center), and Charla Sedacca (right)

Still, in this day of hardcore bodybuilding, the majority of people don't aspire to the level where they want to enter contests. Not only is it too much work, they just don't want huge muscles like a competitive bodybuilder's. What they want is a firm, well-proportioned physique, but they often fail to define exactly what they want to look like. If you're a woman, do you want a chorus girl's body? Or do you want to look like Cory Everson?

When men tell me that they don't want to look like Arnold Schwarzenegger, but they would like to get rid of their beer bellies, I usually suggest that they *stop drinking beer*! I then go on to describe the kind of physique they want but can't express in so many words, trying to give the impression of lean, sinewy, rock-hard muscle.

You can't suddenly throw yourself into an all-out program to lose weight. Never cut your calories drastically, nor increase your training excessively. Dieting and training should be gradual and methodical. Crash diets and blitz programs almost guarantee failure.

Decrease your calories by only 300 calories a day, and stay at that level for at least twenty days. Then assess your progress and make another moderate adjustment. You will probably have to cut another 300 calories, depending on what progress you are making. Remember, an overweight body made that way by years of inadequate exercise and poor nutrition cannot be blitzed into shape by a crash diet, nor hammered into condition by lengthy, over-strenuous workouts. You may want instant results, but you cannot have them.

What I can promise you is excellent rewards if you keep to the suggested regimen. Keep to your plan and six months down the road, you could totally transform yourself. Check out the Chapter on nutrition for muscle mass in this book. The same type of foods also apply to those who want to lose weight—only the amounts vary. Eat moderate servings of protein and carbohydrates. Cut out table salt, sugar, sauces, and gravies. Avoid all deep-fried foods and processed, sugar-loaded goodies. Drink plenty of water and limit your fat intake. Even dieters should have more than three meals a day. Try five or six small meals, but limit the amount of food according to your plan. If you leave the table feeling stuffed, you will gain fat. Leave feeling slightly hungry and you will lose weight.

The pre-exhaust routine that you use to reduce your body weight must serve two purposes: It must tone every muscle in your body, and it must burn calories more quickly than a regular routine.

For this reason, it is suggested that you follow a program of strict exercise style. Neither bounce the weight, nor arch your body to lift heavier poundages. Most importantly, as your body gets used to the program, *decrease* your rest time between every set. Your aim is to create an aerobic effect with your training. Don't allow your heart rate to return to its resting state until the complete workout is finished.

Once you achieve a better level of fitness, begin your next set before breathing returns to normal. In this way, your overlapping oxygen debt will help burn adipose tissue. It will also serve to speed up your metabolism. If you're basically endomorphic, which means that you have big bones, carry a lot of weight naturally, and have a slow

Brad Verret has plenty of room for alternate dumbbell raises.

metabolism, you may want to increase your exercise program by including two or three sessions of traditional aerobic activities every week.

## Walking

Walking burns fat very efficiently. Start by walking at a comfortable pace for your current age and condition. Don't walk long distances unless you're ready for them. As you increase your fitness, swing your arms in an exaggerated manner, and lengthen your stride to its limit. You may later want to hold small dumbbells or wear ankle and wrist weights. It's far better to walk three miles, swinging your arms and stretching your stride, than to walk a mile using ankle and wrist weights. Make sure before you start out that you wear very comfortable shoes and suitable clothing for the weather conditions. You don't want to get cold or wet enough to catch a bad cold or the flu; then you'll miss more than a few workouts. On the other hand, cases of heat stroke have occurred with walkers who wore too much clothing to induce excessive sweating. Be sensible. Find out exactly what the weather is like outside before you leave the house.

## Jogging and Running

Jogging or running for the same amount of time does expend more calories than walking. If you can do it comfortably, all the better. But it is sometimes too demanding for individuals who are unfit, too heavy, too old, or generally not used to the activity. The damage that jogging or running can cause your hip and knee joints from the high-impact pounding is a known fact. Foot and ankle problems can also be aggravated. Do not make a habit of running on uneven or hilly ground.

## Indoor and Outdoor Cycling

Stationary-bike riding at home or in a gym is a very controlled way of burning calories, and as such is highly recommended. Because the pedalling action is usually very smooth, there's very little chance of damaging your joints. It's also a good idea to begin a workout with a period of stationary-bike riding to warm up your muscles and cardiovascular system. The single drawback to burning off fat by riding a stationary bike is boredom. Some

Veronica Dahlin demonstrates the single-arm dumbbell lateral raise.

80

Joanne McCartney isolates her pectorals with cable crossovers.

Hannie Von Aken

trainers get around this by reading or watching television while they pedal those calories into the sunset.

Cycling in the countryside is frequently more stimulating to the body and mind, but drawbacks outdoors are falling off your bicycle and getting hit by a car. Statisticians tell us that every mile we cycle increases our chances of being hit by a careless driver. However, if you want to include outdoor cycling in your exercise program, travel on roads that have little traffic or in a local park and always wear protective clothing and a helmet. My advice is to begin every workout with a ride on a stationary bike.

## Rope Jumping

Few people realize that rope jumping is extremely strenuous. I remember reading once that a famous boxer in preparation for a big fight had managed to jump rope for nineteen minutes. This, his trainer said, was a monumental feat. I regarded it as very ordinary until I took up rope jumping myself. I was totally exhausted after just six minutes!

Rope jumping rapidly accelerates your pulse and raises your metabolism. For that reason, it should only be performed by those who have achieved a good level of cardiorespiratory fitness. You won't be able to rope jump for long periods; consequently, the fat-burning effect may not be as beneficial as other activities. Some aerobic experts prefer to jump rope in sets, each lasting three to five minutes.

## Cellulite

This is a problem that affects women in general, and female bodybuilders are no exception. Some who train regularly, including an aerobic program of exercise still have trouble reducing cellulite on their thighs and hips. It can be worked off, but it takes time and persistence to get rid of it.

Cellulite is nothing more than fat, thick fat, which puckers up and gives that orange peel look to your flesh. Continue with your weight training. If you run for part of your aerobic routine, don't run all-out for short bursts. It's better to walk fast or jog slowly for longer periods of time. When you try to burn energy all at once, you don't burn fat as efficiently as when you work for longer periods at less intensity. Your diet must be tightened up even further. Don't eat junk foods, and make a very special attempt to cut down on saturated and poly-unsaturated fats. Keep table salt out of your diet, and make sure you're getting plenty of vitamins and minerals, with an emphasis on vitamin C. Remember, it takes time, but you can do it!

The following pre-exhaust routine should be performed approximately three times a week. Rather than train your whole body in one workout, which is acceptable if you have the time and the energy, it's usually more convenient to split the routine into two equal parts, performing each part on consecutive days. You can rest every two days, four days, or every five days. The ultra-enthusiast may choose to train six days a week, resting only on Sundays. This is pretty grueling, and usually proves too tiring for most people, but it's an option for the keenest and fittest among you.

### The Weight-Loss Pre-Exhaust Routine

*Deltoids*
Seated Dumbbell Lateral Raise
Wide-grip Barbell Press
*Thighs*
Thigh Extension
Half Squat
*Leg Biceps*
Standing Leg Curl
Thigh Curl
*Calves*
Seated Calf Raise
Donkey Calf Raise
*Chest*
Pec-Deck Flye
Supine Dumbbell Bench Press
*Abdominals*
Crunch
Hanging Knee Raise
*Back*
Bent-arm pullover
Lat-machine Pulldown
*Biceps*
Preacher Bench Curl (90°)
Under-grip Chin-Up
*Triceps*
Cable Pressdown
Close-grip Bench Press

Janice Graser

Ron Love

# 8
# EATING FOR MASS
## Positive Nutrition

Let me begin by confirming that I believe correct nutrition is vital to all bodybuilders. It has to be planned and followed through carefully. You cannot approach modern nutrition carelessly.

Even before this century began, the bodybuilders of the day believed in the importance of nutrition. Their main thrust of endeavor was to hoist large weights over their heads. Their musculature, which they were proud of, was nevertheless a secondary accomplishment. They were considered to be excessively vain if muscular development was the sole reason for training. Their muscles were well deserving of enthusiastic praise, but the focus was on their strength and lifting ability. These old-timers believed in good nutrition, but they were terribly misinformed. Some of them actually believed that the best food was beer!

Before World War II, the ideal strength-building meal was considered to be steak and eggs. Many athletes ate this favorite combination prior to competition.

After the war, with no thanks to Bob Hoffman of the York Barbell Company, bodybuilding started to become accepted. Hoffman was from the old school, which contended that muscles meant nothing unless a man could make a creditable total

Peter Hensel

on the three Olympic lifts: standing press, snatch and clean and jerk. It mattered not one iota that most bodybuilders were far stronger than Olympic lifters in movements like bench presses, curls, and squats, not to mention the dozens of isolation exercises such as leg curls, lat pulldowns, calf raises, thigh and triceps extensions. The Olympic power men couldn't begin to compete with the bodybuilders' strength and stamina in these exercises.

The point is: Bodybuilding could stand on its own as a sport. The iron men were not ashamed to admit that they were, first and foremost, bodybuilders—people who wanted to shape and build their bodies. It was during these post-war years that would-be physique champions wanted to make sure that they were getting all the necessary ingredients for growth, so they ate everything they could get their hands on. Maybe it was a reaction to the food shortages during the war. It was known as the "bulk craze." The most popular food for bodybuilders was none other than milk.

Today bodybuilders have largely abandoned the practice of bulking up to achieve mass because so much of what they gain is fat, which is only desirable if it's needed for insulation. This would be true for long-distance swimmers. Strength is increased with the addition of fat, since it cushions the muscle base, but bodybuilders don't look better with the addition of fat under their skin.

Bodybuilding expert Bill Dobbins said: "Bodybuilders don't believe in bulking up any more, not because it doesn't work. It does work, but at a price. When you let your body weight ascend twenty, thirty, or forty pounds over your contest weight, a lot of that extra bulk is fat, not muscle. So bulking up really means getting fat."

There are several reasons why we should never allow our bodies to gain too much fat.

1. Fat fills in the valleys and lines between the muscle groups and flattens peaked biceps, reduces back definition, and hides the abdominals, sometimes to the extent that none of these muscles can be seen at all.
2. Fat contributes to poor health. It increases the likelihood of numerous diseases, including stroke, diabetes, heart attack, and cancer.
3. Being considerably overweight makes it difficult to rip up at contest time. You are faced with the unenviable catch-22 situation of having to *starve* your body to lose fat, yet *feed* it to maintain mass.

Aaron Baker and Veronica Dahlin

Look at the bulk of Californian Brad Verret.

When you train hard, you create a demand for nutrients in your body. You have to fill that demand as precisely as you can, which means to supply the correct ingredients in the right amounts. If your body doesn't get enough nutrients, growth can be slowed down or even come to a halt. If you overfeed your muscles with proteins, fats, or carbohydrates, you will likely get fat! I'm not suggesting that you count every calorie, nor that you tear your hair out trying to figure out exactly what nutrients you need, but there's a happy medium. You may not be able to be scientific to the last gram, but you should *not* eat indiscriminately when it comes to your nutrition program.

Dr. Fred Hatfield replied to the question: Why are bodybuilders today bigger and more cut with muscle definition? "Scientific training plus carefully *controlled* supplementation and diet equals improved nutrient utilization and tissue recuperation for elevated anabolism that leads to greater mass."

High-calorie intake alone, despite what some champions may tell you, is not the answer. Training and resting regularly while consuming loads of food will bulk you up, but it will not make you a great bodybuilder. If you consume 3,500 more calories each day than your body needs, you'll gain roughly a pound of fat a day. Eating adequate amounts of complex carbohydrates and protein when combined with tough, pre-exhaust training will give you muscle.

How much should you eat? Actual amounts, of course, depend upon your sex (men usually need more food than women), your weight, your metabolic rate (fast metabolisms require more food, slow ones need less), and your age. Less food is required for people over thirty years of age. Teenagers and those in their early twenties usually require plenty of nourishment. Trainers who perform long and demanding routines require more than those who do short or infrequent workouts. Your vocation also has an effect on your eating habits. If you work at a manual-labor job, you must eat more frequently if you want to gain muscle mass.

## Breakfast

There are a million variations of foods that can help us gain mass. Let's look at the traditional breakfast. It consists of strong coffee, juice, bacon, fried eggs, home fries, and white toast with butter and jelly. It may taste good, but it's hardly the kind of nourishment that will pack on inches of shoulder, arm, chest, and leg muscles. Try hot oatmeal, which many bodybuilders are including in their breakfasts. Marjo Selin and Cory Everson are oatmeal advocates, but Britishers Al Beckles and Reg Park were eating it to build muscle over forty years ago! If you don't like it, then try a bowl of natural muesli, which is made up as follows:

2 cups oat flakes
½ cup dried fruits (dates, apricots, raisins)
¼ cup slivered unsalted nuts (almonds, walnuts, cashews)
¼ cup sunflower seeds
1 tablespoon wheatgerm
2 tablespoons bran
¼ cup safflower oil
½ cup honey

John Terilli

Anita Gandol

Mix the dry ingredients together in a large bowl, then spread on a baking sheet. Pour over the safflower oil mixed with the honey. Bake in a 300-degree oven for about forty-five minutes, let cool, and store in an airtight container. This is enough for four generous servings.

Another alternative would be a large bowl of fat-free, sugar-free yogurt mixed with sliced fruits such as bananas, peaches, pears, apples, and oranges.

For the high-protein part of your breakfast, I suggest eggs, because they have been proven to be the highest-quality protein known to mankind. Every other protein food is rated against the egg! Don't fry or scramble them in butter. Eggs already contain loads of fat in the yolks and should be either boiled or poached. It's a good idea to eat only one yolk for every three or four egg whites. This will keep your cholesterol level down.

Want to have a real stoked breakfast? Try adding some whole-wheat toast with sugar-free preserves. Or add a dish of fresh fruit salad. For a thirst-quencher, freshly squeezed fruit juice, herbal tea, or plain water.

Albert Beckles (left) and Bob Paris

## Lunch

The average lunch is pitiful: a hamburger and fries, or canned soup and a hot dog. All deep-fried foods are out. Make a habit of eating fried foods every day and you're dead in the water. An ideal lunch would consist of tuna or chicken salad, whole-wheat pita bread, fresh fruit, and iced or herbal tea. Again, there are scores of variations for a bodybuilder's lunch. Other examples could be broiled fish with steamed vegetables, turkey, cold cuts with raw carrots, celery, and grapes. Alter-

natively, a half cup of low-fat cottage cheese with whole-wheat bread and tomatoes would be a wise choice if you're trying to lose body fat.

## Dinner

Traditional America eats steak and potatoes for its evening meal and, of course, the old standby, apple pie. British people are more sensible: They have a lighter meal at supper, preferring, like so many Europeans, to have a heavier lunch.

Health-minded bodybuilders should consider grilled fish or calf's liver, fresh vegetables (cabbage, cauliflower, broccoli, or beans), and a garden salad. Finish with fresh fruit, such as pineapples (chock full of enzymes), pears, peaches, or grapes. And yes, if you must, conclude with a small black coffee.

Chicken breasts and rice make another great supper-time alternative, or you could try lamb or beef with boiled potatoes and salad. The important point is that you eat well. Don't spoil the effect by adding salt, sauces, gravies, ketchup, or calorie-dense foods like cakes, cookies, chocolates, butter, sugar, canned soups and fruit, jelly, soft drinks, processed cheese, potato chips, crackers, ice cream, and virtually all processed convenience-store specials.

For ambitious bodybuilders who are trying to gain weight, eating three square meals a day is *not* enough. Six is a better number, which means adding three mini-meals between breakfast and lunch, midafternoon, and before you go to bed. Ideal snacks consist of fresh fruits, raw vegetables with low-fat meat or cheese, dried fruits and nuts, natural vegetable soups, frozen low-fat yogurt, skim or low-fat milk and boiled eggs. Never eat right before a workout, and never eat so much that you feel stuffed or overfull. Here is some basic dietary information to help you be more selective in building maximum muscle mass with minimum amounts of body fat.

# Protein

You will need to consume almost a gram of protein per pound of lean mass body weight every day. Calculate this according to your best contest weight if you are currently in a bulked-up state. When you are trying to develop muscle mass most meals or snacks should contain at least twenty grams of protein. Remember, protein is the substance that actually builds and repairs your muscle cells.

# Carbohydrates

Think of carbohydrate not only as fuel, but as a way to bigger muscles. Your muscle cells cannot easily grow without plenty of complex carbs. Needless to say, like protein, excess carbs can lead

to the storage of body fat, but it's important to have some carbohydrates with every protein food so your body can metabolize it properly. It's not healthy to eat protein by itself. A large variety of carbs is preferable, with plenty of fruits, starches, pasta, and grains to ensure adequate levels.

# Fats

Keep fats to a minimum. Many foods contain fats, and some are necessary for good health, but don't make a habit of eating high-fat cheese, butter, cream, or mayonnaise. Always trim fat from meats. Even lean meats contain sufficient fat for your body's essential requirements. Remember, fats contain more than twice as many calories per gram as protein or carbohydrates. A diet low in fat is important to keep your body fat low while gaining mass.

# Salt

Almost every food contains salt, and you generally ingest far too much of it. When we get too much in our diets, it can lead to edema, amounting to several pounds of water. But worse than that, salt can damage your kidneys, cause high blood pressure, and even increase your likelihood of heart problems. The Heart Association of America recommends one gram of sodium per 1,000 calories consumed, and no more than three grams daily. Actually, you can keep healthy on only 600–800 milligrams of sodium daily, yet you may be consuming twenty to thirty times that amount. Salt occurs naturally in fruits, vegetables, nuts, meats, and eggs. It's even in our drinking water. Never use table salt in a shaker to add it to a meal. It's just too much. Start using no-salt seasonings today. You'll be healthier for it.

# Milk

Milk is about 87 percent water, but it contains over 100 identifiable components including protein, fat, carbohydrates, vitamins, minerals, and trace elements. It is considered an almost perfect food. After all, all mammals gain large amounts of body weight from birth drinking nothing but milk. Very thin bodybuilders would do best by drinking whole milk; those who want mass with less fat

Gary Strydom

should drink low-fat milk (2 percent) or skim milk, which has no fat.

Some people cannot digest milk, because they lack the enzyme called lactase. Many Asians and blacks have lactase intolerance. When you don't have the lactase enzyme in your digestive system, the milk sugar you consume begins to ferment in your stomach. You could get an upset stomach, including cramps and diarrhea. Today many supermarkets supply milk that has been treated with lactase to allow full digestion to take place.

Don't stray from this advice. Junk foods, and poor nutrition will take a toll on your body. High-quality foods in their natural, unprocessed condition will bring you bodybuilding success. Go for it.

Rich Gaspari struts his stuff with Berry DeMey looking on.

# 9
# REST AND RELAXATION
## How Much for Growth?

Two all-time great bodybuilders, though essentially from different eras, were Reg Park and Arnold Schwarzenegger. Each has given literally thousands of exhibitions and seminars around the world. And that type of schedule always involves irregular hours. Frequently, one only manages to get four or five hours of sleep at night, sometimes less. Things were no different for Reg Park and Arnold Schwarzenegger; they seldom enjoyed the luxury of sleeping a full eight or nine hours during their extended tours. At the same time, both men were up at the crack of dawn to train. They never missed workouts.

Getting insufficient sleep, however, is *not* the way to maximize progress. Admittedly, both Schwarzenegger and Park didn't seem to suffer, but both men are genetic superiors when it comes to suitability to the sport of bodybuilding. How much sleep and rest do you need? The normal requirement for human beings ranges about eight hours, but there is practical evidence to suggest that for hard-training bodybuilders, men and women who want to reach their goals as quickly as possible, eight hours of sleep per night may not be enough!

Finland's Marjo Selin can't wait to get to the gym.

Peter Hansel, Lee Haney, Mike Christian, Berry DeMey, and Rich Gaspari join hands on stage.

Beautifully muscled Finnish bodybuilder Marjo Selin frequently has to make do with only a few hours of sleep during her seminar tours, but, like Arnold and Park, she never misses workouts. Even so, she's the first to admit: "Good, solid sleep should be top priority with all bodybuilders, especially those who are desperately trying to add muscle mass. You are definitely putting excessive strain on your metabolism when you get insufficient sleep and rest—certainly enough to prevent muscle growth."

## Recuperation

Recuperation takes place during sleep. You may not recuperate fully overnight, but at least 80 percent of that recovery is your goal. If you miss this target, you run the risk of leaving your body vulnerable to illness and disease. Exhaustion makes you more susceptible to the usual run of viruses, bacteria, and overtraining symptoms. As

Armand Tanny, Mr. U.S.A., explains: "Regular, sufficient sleep is a critical component of training. Many top bodybuilders consider it a bigger factor than diet and even training itself."

Sleep helps us heal. When a bodybuilder obtains less sleep and rest than his body needs, he's inadvertently introducing a negative factor into his lifestyle. The hard-training bodybuilder with the highest-quality genetics and the least amount of negative lifestyle habits is the person who will win the top trophies. Other obvious drawbacks are smoking, alcohol consumption, irregular training, partying, mental stress, excessive physical activity, and poor nutrition. Even if you have no unhealthy habits, bear in mind the importance of regular, sound sleep. It restores your body's red blood cells, damaged tissues are renewed, and mental faculties are regenerated.

Don't underestimate the magical qualities of sleep. During the early part of the sleep cycle, an essential growth hormone is released into your system. No wonder so many successful bodybuilders take a nap during the day. Every time they do, that growth hormone is automatically injected into their systems.

Experts haven't even discovered what makes sleep so vital. Tests have shown that after being deprived of sleep, people can't even think straight, let alone perform well physically. No scientist has come up with an ideal sleep allocation, though most admit that seven or eight hours sleep per night is a ballpark figure. Some experts emphasize that a good night's sleep is whatever makes you feel refreshed, ambitious, and alert the next day.

## How Much Sleep Is Enough?

It's true that we all need different amounts of sleep; some of us require seven hours nightly while others do best on ten hours. But the reality is that unless our lifestyle is completely controlled to the point of being identical from one day to the next, our sleeping requirements vary. As an experienced bodybuilder, you'll find that on days following a really heavy or prolonged workout, you'll need up to ten hours to get refreshed. On the other hand, on mornings following a rest day, you may find that you can't sleep more than six hours.

According to studies, two-thirds of Americans sleep seven to eight hours per night; one-fifth of them sleep less than six hours and one-tenth sleep more than nine. Studies show that too little sleep can cause irritability, weight loss, increased likelihood of illness, mental anxiety, and drowsiness. Excessive sleep can lead to lethargy, heart problems, weakness, and obesity. One Stanford University study found that when students were permitted to select their own sleeping habits, they elected to sleep longer than seven to eight hours. This statistic may have little significance, because lying in a warm bed may be preferable to sitting in a classroom situation where one is constantly expected to be alert and informed.

People can still perform well physically and mentally when deprived of some sleep. It's also interesting to note that sleep lost can be made up to some extent. Further, it's also true that your body can adjust to getting less sleep than it did previously. What is universally agreed upon is the fact that we all need some sleep, in spite of a few individuals who claim that they only need an hour or two a night. Those who have a great deal less than the average become sick. Bodybuilders who train hard four, five, or six days a week need more than seven to eight hours a night.

Sleep consists of two distinct phases: dream sleep and deep sleep. Scientists tell us that deep sleep is the type we need most; and it always comes during the first half of our normal sleep cycle. Surprisingly, most of us get only about 45 minutes of deep sleep each night. This may account for the effectiveness of short naps that so many top bodybuilders are noted for taking. In my bestselling book *Beef It!* (Sterling Publishing Co., Inc., New York, NY), I opened a few eyes, so to speak, in my original Chapter, "The Muscle Sleep." I explained how a high percentage of professional bodybuilders took afternoon naps, a practice that they found essential for maximum muscle recuperation.

As a practicing bodybuilder, whether you have great potential or not, you owe it to your health and well-being to get regular, sound sleep each night. The idea of taking an afternoon nap is unrealistic for most working people. I have to admit that although I have been training regularly for over thirty years, I could never forfeit two or three hours in the afternoon to unconsciousness. On the other hand, if you are a professional bodybuilder who depends on the sport for a living, there's a case for using "muscle sleeps" to improve your progress. It's also important to go to bed at the same time each night, which enables your internal clock to adjust. Most bodybuilders do this instinctively, especially when an important contest is on the horizon.

It's not a good idea to train late at night. The strenuous activity interferes with your metabolism's natural inclination to slow down in preparation for deep sleep. Training before bedtime stimulates your body's chemistry. This has the effect of waking you up rather than preparing you for rest, relaxation, and peaceful slumber. If you have difficulty sleeping at night, avoid taking sleep-inducing pills, which could become a dangerous habit. It's better to take a warm bath and eat a light snack. Traditional sleep-inducers are warm milk, bananas, and cereals. Frank Zane took the amino acid tryptophan to help induce slumber. It activates the production of serotonin, which is essential for deep sleep, by inhibiting chemicals in your brain that keep you awake.

You get the idea. Regular, sound sleep is important for effective musclebuilding. Sweet dreams!

98

Hammer curls for the forearms and lower biceps belted out by John Terilli.

Luiz Freitas

# 10
# AMINO ACIDS
## The Essence of Life

The hype over amino acids is still raging. Any bodybuilder worth his salt is aware that amino acids are the building blocks for muscle proteins. They feed the entire muscular system.

But there's lots more. True, amino acids nourish and help your muscles grow bigger, but did you know that they're also instrumental in mobilizing body fat? Plus, they can stimulate vital growth-hormone release. And that spells, in no uncertain terms, *mass*, truly every male and female bodybuilder's dream word.

Amino acids in protein are split into two distinct groups: essential and non-essential. Actually, you need all the known amino acids, but the *essential* ones are those that aren't manufactured by your body. The non-essential category can be manufactured by your body in sufficient amounts.

Perhaps the most exciting news in the world of nutrition and bodybuilding is the fact that growth-hormone stimulation can be heightened by the supplementation of certain amino acids. This has resulted in a whole slew of manufactured products that capitalize on the scientific research done in the early 1980s. How do they work? Scientists are not sure of all the details, but there has

Who's that showing some thigh? Gary Strydom.

been conclusive proof that amino acids of the right combination and in sufficient dosage stimulate your pituitary gland to secrete H.G.H. (growth hormone), which in turn directly affects growth patterns, muscle hardness, strength development, and fat mobilization.

Dr. Fred Hatfield is without doubt a recognized expert on the subject of amino-acid supplementation and muscle and strength development. He states: "A protein molecule cannot be manufactured by the body unless all the required amino acids are present. In fact, all amino acids must be at the site of protein synthesis before any of them can act."

This means that every essential amino acid must be present in the food we eat, if protein synthesis is to take place. When a particular meal is lacking in some essential amino acids, the ones consumed are either used as energy or stored in cells, possibly even as fat. They are not useful at that time for significantly increasing muscle mass because the chain is incomplete.

Amino acids are involved in an enormous number of functions that are the essence of life. Without them, we could not survive. They help to regulate our metabolic processes for starters. They nourish blood, regulate nerves, metabolize sugar, generate energy, aid digestion, form antibodies, protect organs, and even control hair growth. Amino acids are involved in practically every body function known.

Enthusiastic bodybuilders, especially those at the early stages of training, may make the mistake of thinking that amino acids alone are the answer to gaining muscle size. This isn't true. It should be remembered that balanced nutrition is a vital part of the entire process. Vitamins, minerals, and other nutrients play a primary role in the total body development and in all metabolic processes. Nutrients interrelate, including amino acids, and this fact should never be forgotten, because without the proper variety and balance, you will not even begin to fulfil your bodybuilding potential.

## A Safe Substitute for Steroids?

In this day and age of wide anabolic-steroid consumption (over 3 million North Americans are estimated to be taking anabolic steroids), amino

102

Juliette Bergman performs the alternate dumbbell curl.

Berry DeMey

Mike Christian (left) and Rich Gaspari

acids offer some hope. If taken in the right amounts and dosage, they're capable of bringing about a similar anabolic effect to that obtained from potentially dangerous drugs. Further, bear in mind that good nutrition, especially when amino-acid supplementation is involved, works best for those bodybuilders who train hard and schedule their sleep and recuperation for maximal effect.

You may well ask: How can I use amino acids to improve the anabolic processes of my body? According to Dr. Fred Hatfield, two hormones are more potent than any others. They are somatotropin, or H.G.H., and insulin. Scientists tell us that neither work particularly well in promoting mass when used alone, but synergistically, they are un-paralleled. Hatfield says: "These nutrients can be

administered in the form of an injectable drug, but the practice is both unnecessary and potentially dangerous. I recommend stimulation by natural means. This has been shown to work extremely well for bodybuilders, in promoting muscular growth, increased tendon and ligament strength, and in the overall reduction of body fat percentage."

H.G.H. release is safely stimulated by arginine, ornithine, cysteine, tryptophan, histidine, and lysine.

Hatfield wrote in Joe Weider's *Muscle and Fitness* magazine: "As for insulin, you needn't worry about its secretion because H.G.H.'s action in sparing glycogen from use as energy concurrently causes greater than normal insulin release."

105

Mike Ashley

## The Amino Acids

There are ten amino acids that cannot be synthesized, or only in insufficient quantities, by your body. They are the essential amino acids. You can manufacture the other amino acids that come under the label of the non-essential variety.

*Essential Amino Acids*
Arginine
Histidine
Isoleucine
Leucine
Lysine
Methionine
Phenylalanine
Threonine
Tryptophan
Valine

*Non-Essential Amino Acids*
Alanine
Aspartic acid
Cysteine
Cystine
Glutamic
Glycine
Hydroxylysine
Hydroxyproline
Proline
Serine
Tyrosine

*Nonprotein Amino Acids*
5-hydroxytryptophan
L-3-4-dihydroxyphenylalanine

*Other Amino Acids*
Ornithine

## Inosine

Recently, there has been quite a substantial amount of attention given to a substance known as inosine. The chemical name for inosine is purine nucleotide. Its function in the body is to metabolize sugar, synthesize protein, and improve respiration to help transport oxygen to the muscle fibers where it can be used for the production of energy. The presence of inosine promotes higher levels of A.T.P. (adinosine triphosphate), which improves muscle contractions. Basically speaking, all this should allow the bodybuilder to work out with more intensity and effectiveness, and, hopefully,

Joe Bucci trains naturally with no steroids.

lead to better results from training.

It's claimed that athletes from Soviet-block countries are using large doses of inosine instead of anabolic steroids, because the use of steroids is banned by the International Olympic Committee. For that matter, Olympic athletes are prohibited from using any kind of performance-enhancing drugs. To my knowledge, many of the athletes are still taking them, and still trying to beat the drug test in a variety of ways. Of course, as the debate about performance-enhancing drugs and steroids continues to develop around the world, the tests to detect drugs in athletes' bodies are becoming more accurate. Indeed, more athletes are getting caught. In the 1988 Olympic Games in Seoul, Korea, Canadian sprinter Ben Johnson was disqualified from winning the 100-meter race after testing positive for steroids in his body.

As to the safeness of taking inosine, there has not been a large number of controlled experiments performed as yet. However, there's some indication that very large amounts could be toxic to your liver. Until more conclusive results are in, it's certainly a risk to take any type of substance artificially. Consult your doctor before experimenting with any type of drug, and be aware of the consequences.

Ming Chew spots Ramona Petty as she performs dumbbell curls.

# 11
# SPOTTING
## The Helping Hand

Ever wonder why those people who train at a gym make faster and better progress than home trainers? Sure, most gyms have expensive machines and equipment. And there are ready-made dumbbells all laid out in pairs from five pounds to five zillion. Certainly, good apparatus helps, but the big boost comes from the assistance you get from fellow gym members. It comes in the form of the helping hand, known in the iron game as spotting.

When you know that someone is standing behind you while you're hoisting iron up and down in the bench press, it gives you three things invaluable to progress. You have *security* knowing that if you fail to lift the weight, it can be handed off in seconds. You have *confidence* in going for a new goal in either reps or poundage; and you have *encouragement* that may be spoken in a few quiet words: "Come on!" "One more!"

There are a few bodybuilders who may feel that spotting is for sissies, that it's not a useful policy to make an exercise easier by having a training partner lift your weight for you. Nothing could be further from the truth. Spotting helps you to extend a set, beyond what you would normally do. Spotting doesn't make training easier. It makes it harder, but more effective. And consequently, those who use training partners to help them increase the intensity of a set invariably end up making better all-around bodybuilding progress.

Marjo Selin (left) aids Tonya Knight in this sequence depicting cable curls.

Carla Dunlap chats with a few fellow trainers.

It's important to keep spotting as an aid to adding more quality reps and heavier work loads in perspective. Use it to help your workouts become more creative. Employ spotting to break down more muscle tissue than you ever thought possible. Remember that a muscle cell either fires off completely or it doesn't at all. The more muscle cells you involve during a set, the more your body is forced to repair and subsequently overcompensate for the stress.

That's why the gym trainer has it over the home trainer, not that every exercise requires a spotter's help. You can work several muscle groups quite adequately in a home gym, with no one else for company other than your mirrored image on the wall. It's not necessary for a spotter on exercises like curls, triceps extensions, abdominal movements, and forearm exercises. But do those multi-joint, heavy-duty movements like the bench press, the squat, and the incline press, and you'll see the reason why a spotter gives an absolute advantage. Even so, don't use a spotter as a crutch. Use one for better workouts, not as an audience for your entire workout.

Negrita Jayde curls her awesome arm.

Rick Valente works as Lorie Innes watches.

## Mixed Training Partners

There has been a trend of late for body-builders to use partners of the opposite sex. At first, this seemed ludicrous. Men, after all, were ten times stronger than women . . . or so we thought. But as females came into the sport, the men slowly began to realize that an athlete is an athlete. Women bodybuilders *could* take the heat. Obviously, there has to be some kind of compatibility between men and women training together. It wouldn't make sense for a man capable of squatting with "six plates" aside to share a heavy leg workout with a beginning female bodybuilder who's only capable of squatting with the bear-

naked bar. For one thing, if he got into trouble trying to surface from a deep squat, she wouldn't be able to offer much help. Then, she'd wear herself out taking all those plates off the bar when it came time for her set of squats!

But, today, it's just as likely that the girl at your neighborhood gym is equally as strong as you are. And as many of you know, there's a host of iron maidens out there who are so powerful, in fact, that men shy away from them for fear of seeming too wimpish! Well, how would you stack up training alongside Dorothy Herndon, Bev Francis, Nichole Bass, or Tonya Knight?

The point is that men and women *can* work well together. So what if they can't always be close

114

on exercises like squats and bench presses. There will be movements that women do that their male counterparts find impossible. Take Matt Mendenhall for example. He trained with Rachel McLish for a while and never could duplicate her leg curls where she brings her thighs right off the bench, lifting the weight ostensibly with her glute muscles. My own editor Greg Zulak was taking his regular workout in Mississauga Gold's, just down the road from MuscleMag's Bodybuilding Store in Bramalea. One of our freelance illustrators, Rose Barros, was training her legs. She invited Greg to spot her on her squats. Now, Rose is a frail-looking, small-boned young lady, so Greg was a little surprised that she performed an initial set with 145 pounds. When she plopped on another couple of plates, making it 245, he gasped in astonishment, but to his utter amazement, for her last set, she went for a mind-boggling 345.

There's some evidence to show that when men and women train together as spotting partners, there's a greater release of hormones, resulting perhaps from trying, however unconsciously, to impress the opposite sex. Most bodybuilders agree that working with the opposite sex stimulates a more serious effort to try harder, which is what success is usually about.

Curiously enough, one-on-one training, which is so popular today, doesn't always involve spotting techniques. In fact, I have seen so-called trainers who have refused to even count reps for their clients, even though they charge $50 an hour for their services. The originator of one-on-one training was Vince Gironda. Many moons ago, he would charge actors a substantial fee to put them through a workout. Vince had the right idea, too. He trained with his client. This enabled the workout to be paced properly, and kept the client actively involved from beginning to end. Franco Columbu, who has personally trained stars like Sly Stallone, agreed with this technique. He said: "I always train with my client. I need to feel part of the training session, so I get totally involved and train, too."

## Forced Reps

Every lift you do, every exercise, has a section of the movement that is the hardest to perform. Take the curl, for example. The hardest part is when your forearms are parallel to the floor. Once

Bertil Fox is all muscle!

Tonya Knight (left) spots Marjo Selin in the hanging leg raise.

you're past it, the lift becomes easier. When you bench press, about halfway up, the weight seems real heavy. Get past that point and completing the lift is easy. Here's where the spotter comes in. By placing the fingers of both hands under the bar and gently directing the weight upward, the spotter can "help" the exerciser past the sticking point of an exercise. Without this help, the trainer wouldn't be able to perform another repetition, and the set would have ended.

You can see clearly how a good spotter can extend a set by several repetitions; usually two or three extra reps are adequate. When a barbell is used in exercises like incline presses, press behind neck, standing curls, and bench presses, both hands should be placed under the bar. In dumbbell movements, because you don't want to tip or unbalance the weights, it's usually advisable to place your hands under the trainer's elbows.

## Negative Reps

The negative part of a repetition is when you lower the weight. Thirty years ago, Art Zeller—then a famous bodybuilder, now a famous photographer—used to hoist a heavy dumbbell to his shoulder, place his elbow inside his hip joint, lean backward, and slowly fight the weight as it lowered (uncurled) to the straight-arm position. In other words, it was too heavy to curl so he got into the finished position of the curl and gained the benefit by lowering the weight through the curling path. Hold it! Art also tore his biceps as a result of using enormous weights, so beware of getting too enthusiastic with this form of negative training.

Today bodybuilders use negatives by utilizing spotters who help lift the weight up and allow them to lower slowly without help. In fact, some spotters actively increase negative resistance by adding pressure to make the set tougher. Negatives can be a severe drain on your muscles, so use them only periodically when training for a contest. Too many negative reps in a workout can cause an overtrained condition.

## Triple-Dropping Method

Arnold used this technique in his heyday. It works like this. After warming up, start a set of barbell curls, for example, with maximum weight.

Gary Strydom with his wife, Alyse

117

When you've completed six reps and another one is impossible, have two spotters remove a ten-pound disc from either side simultaneously. Continue with your reps, seven, eight, nine, ten, ouch! Can't do another one? Get rid of two more ten-pounders; eleven, twelve, thirteen, fourteen. That's it! The triple-dropping method is one of the most severe methods of all. It can be used in conjunction with straight sets, supersets or advanced pre-exhaust sets.

Naturally, when triple-dropping with an exercise machine, you only need one partner to pull the pin and reinsert it at a lesser resistance. In fact, some machines are designed so that you can change the resistance while you exercise because the pin and stack are within easy access.

There is no doubt in my mind that a *good*

workout can be made into a *super* workout if your training partner can spot you effectively with sensitivity, encouragement, and perfect timing. The ideal spotting partner doesn't shout; he or she almost whispers. "Two more . . . you can do it! One more . . . nice going!" When a spot is needed, the hands are there. A good spotter anticipates his partner's needs. He edges the resistance upwards—smoothly does it.

A good spotter keeps the exercise rhythm intact. He never allows the resistance to lose momentum and come to a standstill. On the other hand, a spotter should not take on too much of the effort. The helping hand is given before the weight is stopped in its tracks. A spot comes in when the exerciser shows *signs* of failing, not when he or she *actually* fails.

Dave Zelon (left), Sean Ray (center), and Mike Christian

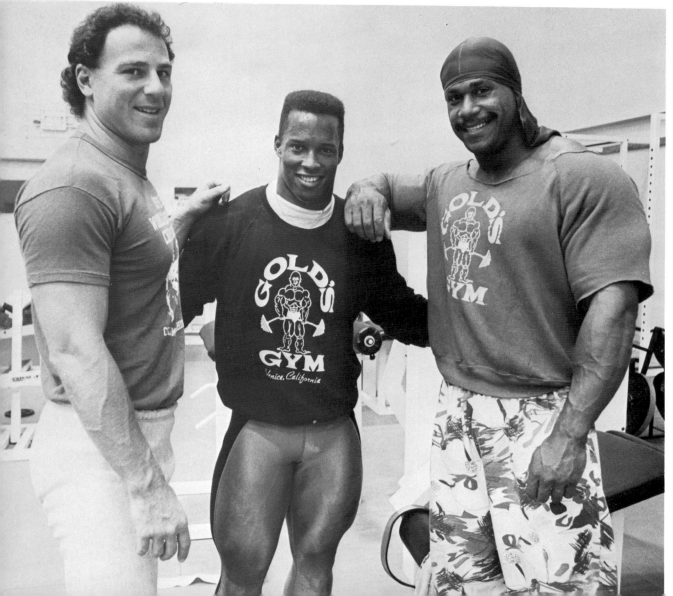

The Dutch girls: Hannie Von Aken (left), Ellen Van Maris (center), and Connie Heusdans (right)

A spotting partner has to keep his thoughts on the job. His mind has to be tuned in to every rep of every set. If your spotting partner is shouting and screaming to get attention for himself, dump him. One of the spotter's duties is to offer encouragement and praise. Correctly chosen words are like magic to the exerciser. You'll get more quality reps as a result.

## Weight Belts

Frequently, you see men and women wearing thick, leather training belts when they work out. Can belts really help prevent injuries? Well, wearing a belt is no substitute for a spotter, but they do provide some benefits.

Originally belts were worn by circus performers to add support when they attempted heavy lifts at fairgrounds and music-hall theaters. When bodybuilding training first became practiced regularly in the thirties and forties, very few belts were used. Today bodybuilders nearly always use belts for heavy squats to give them a tight support around their midsections. Always bear in mind that when you squat your stomach is frequently pushed outward. A tight belt can help you keep control of this abdominal distension. Frank Zane would wear a weight belt backwards with the wide side in front to prevent his stomach from bulging while he squatted. My advice is to wear a belt for rowing, squatting, deadlifting, and all overhead presses. The rest of the time a belt is optional, and purely an individual choice.

John Hnatyshack

# 12
# EIGHT BODY-BUILDING MISTAKES
## The Progress Killers

For a long time now, bodybuilding success has been known to depend on hard training, good nutrition, and sufficient relaxation. But, in reality, there's more to success than just these three simplistic factors. Certainly, none of the three categories can be ignored if your are serious about being the best you can be.

In this Chapter, I will discuss eight common mistakes made by bodybuilders at various times during their training careers. These factors primarily concern training, mental programming, and diet, but I've also touched on something that is more and more common in this sport—steroid abuse.

Double-check your bodybuilding habits and make sure that you're not falling short of your dreams by making one or more of these mistakes.

Tina Plakinger (left) and Reggie Bennett (right) give good support to Rick Valente.

## Ego Maniacs

As a bodybuilder, you're using weights to build and shape your body. You go to the gym to look great, not to demonstrate your strength. Every rep of every set must be performed with building and shaping the muscle in mind. If your object is to build strength, then go for it and become a power or Olympic lifter. Both are worthy sports; but don't expect to have the well-sculpted muscular appearance of a true bodybuilder.

Many times I have seen bodybuilders bouncing heavy weights on their chests while lifting their hips off the bench during supine presses. I've seen cheat curls done with more body motion than a snake swimming in Lake Michigan. Often these people end up with severe tendinitis or serious injuries.

You know that muscles can't see the actual weight being used; they go by *feel*. To be sure, a 100-pound curl performed in good style is more effective than a super-loose 150-pound curl. Your goal is to use challenging weights, but to make the exercise work your muscles in the best way possible. Be the master of your workouts. When you are straining to merely lift a weight, some of your muscle fibers are the master of *you*. They don't have to contract and therefore will not grow in size. When you use lighter resistance, you're in control. You can use that weight as a tool to fatigue your muscles—to burn, blitz, and bomb them to bring results and ultimate glory into your life.

## Irregular Eating Habits

Optimal nutrition is vital to your body. The analogy between yourself and your new car is as old as the hills, yet it's true. Man is far more likely to put top-grade gasoline into his new sports car than he is to feed himself with optimal nutrition. However you look at it, most cars are dead in the water after ten years, yet *you* have to be in top shape for the rest of your life.

Don't eat junk food on a regular basis. Breakfast is still the most important meal of the day. Include a good cereal or hot oatmeal, eggs, whole-wheat bread, and a couple of pieces of fruit. Make it a hearty meal; after all, you've gone without food for at least eight hours. Lunch should be somewhat smaller and dinner smaller yet. Snack between meals on fresh fruits and vegetables, or something

higher in calories if you are trying to gain weight.

Don't get into a situation where you miss breakfast or other meals. If you have a long stretch of work ahead of you, prepare cold cuts, sandwiches, or a protein mix (in a thermos to keep it cool) so that you can have a snack even though you may not be able to take a long break. Read up on bodybuilding nutrition. Bill Reynolds wrote a good book entitled *Supercut* (Contemporary Books). I wrote the very successful *Rock Hard!* (Warner Books) just for bodybuilders, and *Gold's Gym Nutrition Bible* (Contemporary Books) is also a fine publication. My book *Rip Up!* (Sterling Publishing Co., Inc., NY) also contains lots of diet information on losing body fat quickly.

## Unachievable Goals

Forget that thought in the back of your mind of being a ten-time IFBB Olympia winner. It's not a realistic concept, except for gargantuan Lee Haney, who agrees that: "Goal setting gives you a road map to ultimate bodybuilding success."

In your case, you can set goals to be achieved in twelve months, then divide it by three so that each four months you achieve one-third of your plan. Your goals must be realistic. You need success to spur you on to greater efforts. Don't just plan your goals based on poundages used. It's too easy to promise yourself another thirty pounds on your bench press when the only thing that might change is your exercise style. Aim for another inch on your chest, or half inch on your arms. Be realistic, and then achieve your goals. After that, set another goal, and before you know it, you're on the winner's rostrum.

## Steroids Abuse

Ironically, the very chemicals that build muscular bodies also kill them. Anabolic steroid abuse causes, in time, muscular softness to the point where the bodybuilder looks more fat than muscular. Traditionally, bodybuilding has been championed by men and women with wide shoulders and narrow waistlines. They looked fit, lean, and muscular. But steroids have changed all that. Not only does taking steroids increase risk of liver damage, heart attack, diabetes, prostate enlargement, accelerated aging and hair loss, but they puff out

The extraordinary Joanne McCartney reps out with incline bench dumbbell flyes.

your face and bloat your entire body. Heavy steroid takers develop very thick waistlines that hang out like a heavyweight pro wrestler's gut.

Let's assume that you didn't get permanently sick from taking these bodybuilding drugs. You're still going to wreck your physique. They cause you to lose the one thing that bodybuilders are famous for: the "V" shape. Don't allow steroid abuse to ruin your health and distort your body.

## Failing to Train for Proportion

No bodybuilder, male or female, has a physique in which all areas grow at the same rate. In fact, some less fortunate people have body parts that can't be developed at all. Witness those people with skinny lower legs and forearms that just cannot build any appreciable mass. If you're like most people, you will find that you have one or two stubborn areas that grow more slowly than other body parts. This means that after a few months of all-around bodybuilding, you'll start looking somewhat out of proportion. Athletes are well known for having imbalanced bodies. Compare a cyclist's superbuilt legs, for example, with his or her back, chest, and arms. Compare a gymnast's upper body with his underdeveloped legs. The same can happen with your bodybuilding if you don't concentrate on training your less developed areas.

Always start a workout by training your weakest area first. Give it a few more sets, and maybe an additional exercise, so that it is forced to do that additional work. At the beginning of a workout, you are super fresh and enthusiastic. Starting each training session by working your slowest-growing area makes sense. Don't be like 99 percent of bodybuilders who begin their training with their favorite exercise, which just happens to work, in most cases, the easiest area to develop.

Constantly check your body in the mirror. Ask trusted friends. Study photographs. Assess your physique and become self-critical about your proportion. And work to keep your body development in perfect balance.

## Poor Mental Concentration

Mental concentration is practiced by every successful bodybuilder, by every champion athlete, and by every successful leader. You have to

VG CHAMPIONSHIPS

Phil Hill

125

Paul Jean Guillaume, the natural Mr. Universe. Steroids aren't part of his master plan.

apply yourself totally if the job is to get done.

Even before you start a set, you should mentally prepare yourself. Decide how many reps you'll do. Go over in your mind the style you're going to perform, the isotension, the burn. When the set begins, you should lose contact with everyone around you. Forget other people's conversations. You shouldn't hear things like telephones or salutations. Your mind is a wonderful creation. Even the most sophisticated computers can't think in anywhere near the same way as you can. When human beings apply their minds to a physical task, a kind of magic takes place. True athletes know this. Physical effort is taken into a kind of dream world of euphoria and they achieve almost superhuman greatness. Just look at the incredible development on the amazing men and women within these pages. Have you ever seen anything like it? None of it could be achieved without concentrated effort.

## Overtraining

I suppose it could come as a surprise that overtraining can be a problem. Aren't you always trying to increase intensity, blitzing away at your workouts? Don't the scores of bodybuilding books invariably tell you to increase the overload so that your muscles work harder and harder?

Vince Gironda reminds us that overtraining is the most common cause for bodybuilding failure. Yes, training sessions can be too long and involved. This is especially true of young, beginning bodybuilders who are anxious to make the best-possible progress. Their natural enthusiasm and energy levels are enormously high, but the recovery factor fails them. They don't allow enough between-workout rest time for full recuperation. Beginners often read about the various champions' routines in magazines like *Flex* or *MuscleMag International*. But these are seldom the routines the champs used to build their first fifty pounds of muscle.

Even Lee Haney says: "I seldom use more than fifteen sets per body part, yet I see beginners everywhere doing ridiculously long workouts using up to 20 to 25 sets per muscle group. They will never get big following a routine like that."

Hit each body part hard, then leave it alone. Don't get caught up in the zillion-and-one-sets syndrome.

Britain's Ian Dowe

## Not Taking Supplements

It's not that you have to spend enormous amounts of money on musclebuilding supplements, but you do need to make sure that your system is fed high-quality musclebuilding foods. It may not be necessary to take vitamins if you eat a balanced diet, but who can deny the peace of mind that comes with taking a vitamin/mineral pill each day? You *know* you're getting your recommended daily allowance. Other supplements like high-quality protein powders, glandulars, and amino acids are all pure muscle food. They should not be taken all the time, otherwise their special nutritional benefits could lose their effect. Supplements should be consumed for a reason. Take them at a time when you're making a special push for progress, or when you're trying to look your best for an upcoming contest or a vacation in the sun. When you return to off-season training, you can again rely solely on a regular balanced diet. Supplements have more impact when they are taken irregularly, but they should be taken if you want to maximize your mass-building progress.

There you have it. Are you making any of these eight mistakes? If so, take steps to correct your approach and I'll bet that you'll get right back on track.

The splendid torso of California's Bob Paris

# 13
# BODYBUILDING PRO LIFESTYLE
## The View at the Top

Not everyone wants to get into bodybuilding competition, let alone turn professional and compete on the Grand Prix circuit or even the IFBB Mr. Olympia, but this ambition is at the back of many trainers' minds. There's nothing wrong with that, but you must never lose sight of being realistic. Only a favored few can expect to become Olympians in the competitive world of muscle.

How do you get started in competition? Well, this may seem obvious, but first you must build and shape the body to the extent that you merit being in a contest. Start at the lowest level. Even before entering a show, you should attend several local events so that you get an idea of what will be expected of you. Make a point of seeing the prejudging segment as well as the evening performance. Join your local National Physique Committee. You will find information about this association in *MuscleMag International* and *Flex* magazines.

Many bodybuilding gyms post NPC news of upcoming events on their notice boards. Phone or write your local NPC director and request information about upcoming contests. He will be delighted to send you entry forms once you have become a bona-fide member of the organization. Again, do not enter high-caliber physique events unless you have a high-caliber physique. What is expected of you?

Sean Ray compares abs with Phil Hill (right).

## Backstage Contest Itinerary

Take along a comb, a towel, two pairs of pose trunks (in case you get oil on one pair), some almond oil (for your body), a backstage pass, and a razor to take off the odd hair that may be left on your body. Also a pair of rubberized strands for backstage pumping can be useful, especially if available free weights are limited.

## How You Are Judged

Usually, there are seven judges at each competition. Each is required to rank you in order of merit in each of the three posing rounds: the compulsory poses, the relaxed round, and the free-posing round. Your placing is your score for that round.

To circumvent favoritism by any particular judge, both the highest and lowest scores are dropped in each assessment. In the free-posing round, you'll perform your routine alone, but in rounds one and two, you'll be compared directly with your fellow contestants. In these two rounds, you usually begin the judging process by standing alone on center stage, but later it is standard procedure to be called out for comparisons in groups of two to six bodybuilders. The only way that anyone can be fairly and completely assessed is by comparison.

The following subjects are some considerations to help a professional bodybuilder keep a substantial cash flow coming in. Remember, each pursuit takes action and diligence. Just as your muscles will not grow without regular workouts, neither will your bank account increase without conscientious effort.

## Guest Posing

When you start winning contests, especially of national and international caliber, you'll obtain a measure of fame through the various magazines, but it doesn't mean that you'll be plagued by offers to perform guest-posing spots. You have to make your own contacts with gym owners and contest promoters. The vital thing to remember is that you'd better be in shape when you're asked to guest pose; otherwise, you'll never get asked back. Worse, the word will get around to other promoters that you're in the habit of not being in shape for guest-posing spots.

Two other pointers: Be on time to meet your promoter and don't phone him up during the last week and ask for a plane ticket for your wife or girlfriend. One top star did this recently, and when the promoter refused, the star didn't turn up as contracted.

## One-on-One Training

If you ever become a famous pro, a lucrative job awaits you as a personal trainer. This form of work isn't suitable to all. Some professional bodybuilders develop such an attitude that they cannot abide the idea of counting reps and changing weights for others. One of the original one-on-one trainers was Vince Gironda. He would command enormous fees to put a famous actor through a workout four or five times a week to prepare him for specific film parts.

I remember one amusing story involving one of Britain's top bodybuilders, Dave Prowse. He landed the part of playing the awesome Darth Vader in the blockbuster film *Star Wars*. It so happened that an Arab sheik had seen the film and got it into his mind that he had to be personally trained by Darth Vader. Ever ready to gather up the mega-bucks, Dave flew off to the sheik's palace to act as the rich one's personal trainer. The monetary rewards were splendid, but in spite of this good fortune, Prowse missed his native London. He returned with some meager excuse, but was soon summoned back and paid even more handsomely. But, as rich as he was getting, Dave just couldn't hack the lifestyle. Eventually, he told the sheik that his brother would take over his duties as personal trainer. After all, Dave said, "he's the brother of Darth Vader."

The point to remember about personal training is that the pay can vary tremendously. Some trainers charge as little as $10 a workout, while celebrities are frequently charged $50 to $250 per workout. And with Arab sheiks? Well, I guess the sky's the limit.

## Mail Order

Traditionally, bodybuilding magazine publishers and star champions have made substantial amounts of money from selling items by mail. The

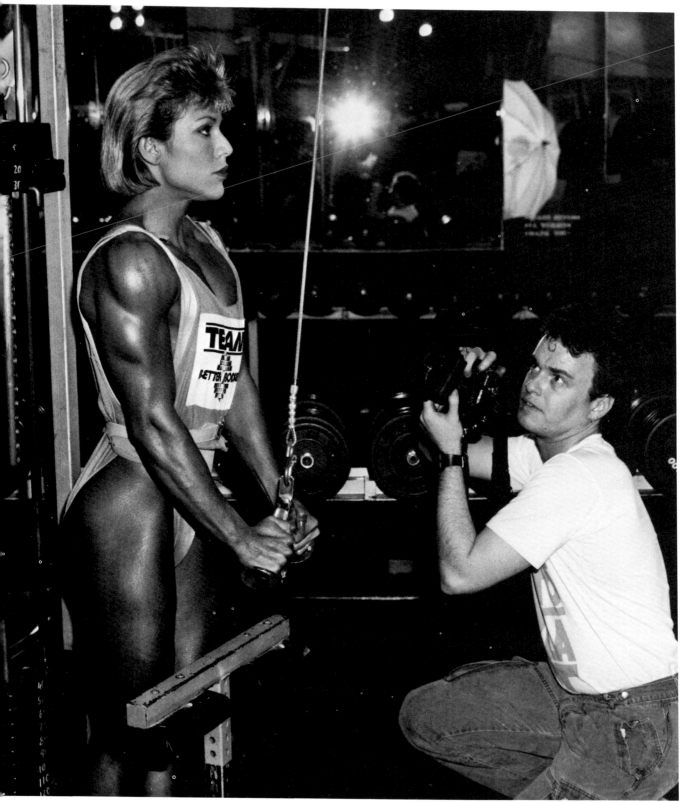

Juliette Bergman completes a triceps pressdown as photographer Steve Douglas records the moment.

products should not be readily available through regular retail outlets, or you'll quickly lose your business. Let me give you an example. When I first started publishing my own magazine, *MuscleMag International*, I sold about a thousand E-Z curl bars each month. Today, because E-Z curl bars are available in almost every well-stocked sporting-goods outlet, my company doesn't average even one mail-order sale of E-Z curl bars per month.

Your product sales are only as good as the advertisement that offers them. Every ad should contain a picture, an exciting headline that catches attention, a subheading, credit-card facilities for phone orders, and an order coupon. The quality of your ad is paramount. A good full-page ad in *Flex* or *MuscleMag International* could pull in over $25,000. A poor ad may only bring in a few hundred dollars.

## Publicity

Doesn't it seem that some people get publicity with enormous ease? I have watched this process over the years and I'm fascinated by it. There's no doubt that certain people attract the press whether they want it or not, but publicity is also the result of hard, continuous self-promotion. Some bodybuilders have a special magic that makes for good press: People like Bob Paris and Anja Langer are eternally sought after by photographers and magazine publishers. They are, after all, beautiful human beings with super shapes and charismatic personalities.

Today, Arnold Schwarzenegger is the champion of the publicity game. He knows how to use the media to his advantage. Arnold first learned the importance of publicity when he returned to his small Munich gym after competing in the NABBA Mr. Universe contest in London. Word had gotten around that he had won the contest, and during the next few weeks, his gym was inundated with people trying to get a look at his 21-inch arms. A sizable amount of those curiosity seekers ended up taking out a gym membership. Arnold saw a direct link between publicity and cash flow that he never forgot.

## Company Endorsements

Arnold Schwarzenegger has endorsed Nike shoes. Cory Everson has promoted Reeboks. And

Bob Paris

scores of other bodybuilders have been paid for endorsing all kinds of products from multi-purpose machines to protein supplements. It goes without saying that your endorsement isn't worth much unless you have built yourself some credibility. You need to be relatively famous, and fame is having people know your name. Curiously enough, although I was never a top competitive bodybuilder, as a publisher and writer, I have built up a certain credibility that has brought me numerous endorsement offers. Unfortunately, I seldom get offered endorsement proposals on products that I truly believe in. Even though the money is good, I have to refuse because I don't feel completely certain that the product is the best available. How do you get paid for endorsing a product? Write to the company, enclosing a photo package of who you are. State your credentials and affirm that you would like to endorse their product because you really do have confidence in it.

Contest-promoting whiz Wayne DeMilia (left) and Dominic Certo congratulate Samir Bannout.

## Books

If you're a big star, chances are that there will be some demand for a book penned by either yourself or a ghost writer. However, being a Mr. or Ms. Olympia is no guarantee that a book will sell. The best-selling books in bodybuilding include Arnold Schwarzenegger's *Education of a Bodybuilder*, Franco Columbu's *Winning Bodybuilding*, and my own *Beef It!* Generally speaking, if a book has loads of up-to-date information, plus at least 200 high-quality pictures, it will sell. How do you get a publisher to publish your book? How much money can you expect? First, who's going to write the book? You may know a lot about training and diet, but can you write about your advice in a competent and readable style? Should you want a professional to write your book for you, then you must expect to share the profits on a fifty-fifty basis. The best professional writers for this job include Joyce Vedral, Bill Reynolds, and myself. Any book that you write has to have its own angle. You cannot hope to sell a book that just repeats the same old stuff. Your book must contain exciting, new information that helps the reader improve his or her physique. Book publishers usually give a cash advance for a manuscript and photos, which varies between $5,000 and $50,000. It's usual to receive a royalty on copies sold of 5 to 8 percent of the retail price of the book, but these royalties don't come to you straight away. They are first applied against the advance until it is paid off in full.

## Bodyguards

More and more bodybuilders are being hired as bodyguards today. Kay Baxter was a bodyguard for Van Halen and made a very good living at it. At one time, Dave Draper did an entire tour with a popular British pop group. Linda Ronstadt always insists on bodybuilder bodyguards: Graham McGregor, owner of Rio Tan, the bodybuilders' favorite tanning facility in Venice, California, was one of her bodyguards. There are endless opportunities if this type of work appeals to you.

## Modeling, TV, and Films

Getting on a local talk show is pretty easy if you're a title-winning professional bodybuilder, but to expand your horizons into the big time is something else entirely. Bodybuilders like Franco Columbu, Steve Reeves, Dave Draper, Reg Park, Ed Fury, Lou Ferrigno, Bob Paris, Tom Platz, Ralph Mueller, and Rachel Mclish have all made good money under the bright lights, not to mention the all-time biggest money-maker, Arnold Schwarzenegger. I think it's fair to say that if you push hard to get a shot at the show-biz way of life, you'll get your chance.

Marjo Selin climbs to the top of the "world."

You can't expect to be cast as Conan the Barbarian if you can't ride a horse. Neither can you expect to be invited back to a soap opera, if you can't summon up at least a modicum of acting ability.

## Magazines

Magazine publishers are in a precarious position. Every month, the print bill is enormous and, needless to say, the issue has to sell in order to make it pay. But there are ways in which professional bodybuilders can help publishers, while at the same time gaining added publicity and increased income.

Publishers are often looking for competent name bodybuilders to write regular columns for their magazines. If they're not in a position to pay cash, an agreement can usually be worked out where the professional is given ad space in the magazine.

When I started *MuscleMag International* in the early 1970s, Arnold would frequently send me photographs to use. He was also quick to point out pictures that I used that he *didn't* like. Today, of course, things have changed. Getting Arnold to pose for a photo session is like pulling teeth.

Photos alone are seldom much use to a magazine publisher. He needs an article to go with them. If you're unable to write, you have to seek out the services of a good writer. Study the magazines to find out the writers who may be interested in writing an article about you for a magazine.

Above all, bear in mind that publishers want to make their magazines as attractive as possible. They won't use pictures or articles unless they are attractive and inspirational. Remember, fame is having people know your name. And in the beginning, at least, much of the process is up to you.

## Photographers

So how do you get publicity? You need to seek out the best photographers in the field. Know them by name. A physique photographer has to be able to pose his models, and he must know the best angles and understand what ingredients make a great photo. Plus, of course, he needs a large amount of technical expertise. The best photographers include John Balik, Steve Douglas, Mike

Neveaux, John Running, Harry Langdon, Greg Aiken, Ralph DeHaan, Chris Lund, and Art Zeller.

If you're already famous or otherwise marketable, these men will gladly photograph you, because they're able to sell the pictures to magazines. But if you're an unknown, you'll have to pay these people to take your photograph, at which time you'll be the owner of the pictures, which you can use as you wish. Make sure that you buy all rights to the photos. Needless to say, when you have pictures taken by a professional, you had better be in top shape, evenly tanned, and prepared to work hard during the session.

## Videos

Making a training video is not all that difficult. Making a top-grade, visually exciting, and informative video is extremely difficult. Try to only work with the best companies. Bear in mind that even a first-rate video will go nowhere unless it has good distribution outlets. There have been numerous videos that went nowhere because there was no "in-place" distribution before it was completed.

## Training Programs

This can be done via mail order or through a particular gym outlet. If you have professional status, other less-successful trainers are often willing to pay for your services in designing their nutrition and training programs. A professional usually charges a consultation fee of $50 to $150 to talk over aspirations, present training techniques, current dietary and exercise habits, at the end of which you design a tailor-made routine and weekly diet program for your client.

## Product Lines

Many wholesale vitamin companies are willing to supply their formulas using your personalized label. They may even make up specific formulas for you. This line can be sold to gyms, health-food stores, and retail outlets such as exercise and sporting-goods stores. Other product lines of your own can include weightlifting belts, T-shirts, sweat suits, and general training apparel, training courses and cassettes.

Bodybuilding pro John Terilli prepares for a photo session with *MuscleMag*'s photographer.

The greatest amateur contest in bodybuilding is the IFBB World Championship.

# 14
# QUESTIONS AND ANSWERS
## Did You Ask?

## Basic Training

**Question:** I know it may sound fundamental to you but I'm a beginner to bodybuilding and I'm not even sure what isolation exercises and combination exercises are. I am anxious to begin the pre-exhaust system because I have heard about the results it can bring. Would you explain the differences?

**Answer:** Isolation exercises work one muscle section only. This doesn't mean that other muscles are not partially involved. It would be impossible to come up with an exercise that didn't involve some other muscles at least peripherally. Most isolation exercises involve the movement of one joint only. Typical examples are concentration curls, thigh curls, triceps extensions, thigh extensions. By contrast a combination exercise works at least two muscle groups. Two or more joints are involved in the motion. A typical example is the bench press. The shoulder and elbow joints are used. The pectorals, shoulders, and triceps are involved strongly. The squat is another example. Not only are the quads worked in their entirety, but the calves, lower back, and glute muscles are also activated. One reason why the squat is considered the king of exercises is that at least three sets of joints are involved: ankles, knees, and hips—and sometimes even the lower back and neck. No wonder a set of twenty squats has you gasping for oxygen!

## Free Weights

**Question:** I train at a spa where they don't have any free weights at all. I like some of the machines, but I have used free weights in the past and I feel I am missing something. I'm serious about making constant improvement and one day I want to compete in bodybuilding competitions. Can you give me your input on this?

**Answer:** Leave the spa. Free weights are where it's at. There are many useful machines that can be an adjunct to your routine, but free weights will be responsible for a good 80 percent of your progress. Take out a membership in a gym that offers plenty of free weights.

## Amino Acids

**Question:** What is meant by "fat mobilization"? I have read this term several times now in connection with amino acid supplementation. Incidentally, since I'm a diabetic, should I take amino acids? Do they change insulin levels in the blood?

**Answer:** Fat mobilization is merely moving fat off your body. It's usually done with a concentrated calorie-reduced diet program. The ideal way, however, is to diet *moderately* while exercising *hard*. As a diabetic, you should be under a doctor's care. Always consult him whenever you make a nutrition or exercise change. Since I'm not a doctor, I cannot offer you advice on how amino acids would affect your metabolism or condition.

## Slippery Grips

**Question:** When my partner and I train, we really work up a sweat. This leads to our hands slipping from the bars when we perform exercises like wide-grip pulldowns, bench presses, chin-ups, rows, or deadlifts. What can we do to solve this?

**Answer:** There are numerous solutions. Go to any sporting-goods shop and buy some chalk. Before you start a lift where you anticipate a problem with a sweaty grip, rub chalk powder on the palms of your hands. If the gym where you train doesn't allow the use of chalk, there are other products available. You can apply a couple of drops of a special solution on each palm before and during training a couple of times as needed. Alternatively, you may find exercise gloves helpful for wide-grip bench presses, and training straps may be the answer when your grip fails on chin-ups, deadlifts, rows, and pulldowns.

## Pre-Exhaust Variation

**Question:** In one of your write-ups about the pre-exhaust system in *MuscleMag International*, you suggested pre-tiring the target muscle with not one, but *three* straight sets of an isolation exercise. Can you please give me a good shoulder routine using this methodology?

**Answer:** This type of training, because it tires out (pre-exhausts) your target muscle even more than one set alternating with a combination exercise, is a method that involves greater stress on your muscle. Consequently, it *may* yield better results. Again, because of the severity of this system, I don't suggest that it be applied to all muscles for every workout.

| Pre-Exhaust Deltoid Routine | | Sets | | Reps |
|---|---|---|---|---|
| Cable Lateral Raise (isolation) | | 3 | × | 10 |
| Dumbbell Lateral Raise | Alternate | 3 | × | 12 |
| Barbell Press Behind Neck | | | | |

## Asymmetrical Muscle Development

**Question:** I have been bodybuilding for two years now. I have made good progress, but lately I have noticed that one of my pectoral muscles is definitely bigger than the other. What can I do?

**Answer:** It's possible that you have suffered a slight tear in your pectoral, so you should consult your doctor. He may advise surgery to correct the problem. However, the vast majority of people who complain of this problem have not torn their muscles at all. When a person notices that he or she has a body part or muscle that is asymmetrical with the other, it is nearly always a very minor difference that no one else notices. Personally, I have never seen a bodybuilder with perfect muscle symmetry. Every one has arms, pecs, lats, and legs of different shapes and sizes.

# Injuries

**Question:** I recently had an elbow injury. The pain is bad, and I cannot straighten my arm. My doctor told me to rest because it was "tennis elbow." I don't play tennis. Can you tell me about my injury?

**Answer:** The condition is known as epicondytitis. The nagging pain can totally immobilize your arm. It's usually situated on the lateral or outer part of your elbow joint. Repeated strain and overuse of your forearm extensor muscles causes it. Several exercises commonly produce this condition, such as close-grip upright or T-bar rowing. If you are susceptible to this problem, perform your rows with a shoulder-width grip to minimize the strain on your forearms. The best treatment is R.I.C.E. (*Rest*, *Ice*, *Compression*, and *Elevation*). Put your arm in a sling with an ice pack. Bandage the area to avoid unnecessary movement. Consult your doctor.

# Judging Contests

**Question:** I have been to many bodybuilding shows and, quite frankly, I'm disgusted at the judges' decisions. The right man or woman seldom seems to win. Since there are all types of sophisticated applause meters available, why don't promoters let the audience decide who is the winner of a contest?

**Answer:** The audience is usually neither qualified nor in the best position to judge a bodybuilding contest. Judges are invariably skilled and versed in the finer points of bodybuilding. Most are extremely experienced in judging and assessing physiques. Additionally, they have front-row seats which gives them the best advantage for noting detail and finer points that are missed by those sitting further back.

Judges make their decisions with the help of judging sheets and score cards that enable them to organize their thoughts and decisions. This is of paramount importance when placing bodybuilders in order of merit, especially lower down the scale. Do you really think that applause meters are going to place bodybuilders fairly when it comes to tenth or even twentieth placings?

Frequently, audiences are made up of people

Mike Ashley

who have never even seen a contest before. Applause meters calibrated to audience response have been used with poor results. Often the person who does the highest number of "most muscular" poses wins. Whereas I agree that current judging methods could be improved upon, I firmly believe that the best man or woman usually wins, especially in the IFBB professional shows and the national NPC events.

# INDEX

# Books by
# Robert Kennedy

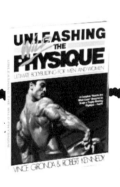